"That love is inexhaustible, you will be there"

forever

_____

_____

_____

_____

_____

THIS BOOK Belongs to

_____

_____

Visit Our Author Page At
amazon.com

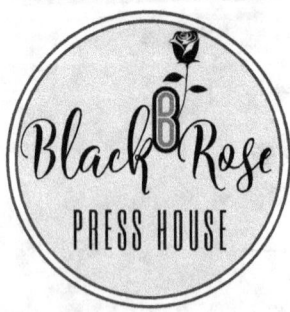

All rights reserved. No part of this book may be used or reproduced in any manner whatsoever without written permission except in the case of brief quotations embodied in critical articles and interviews.

© by BLACK ROSE PRESS HOUSE

Color This Snail

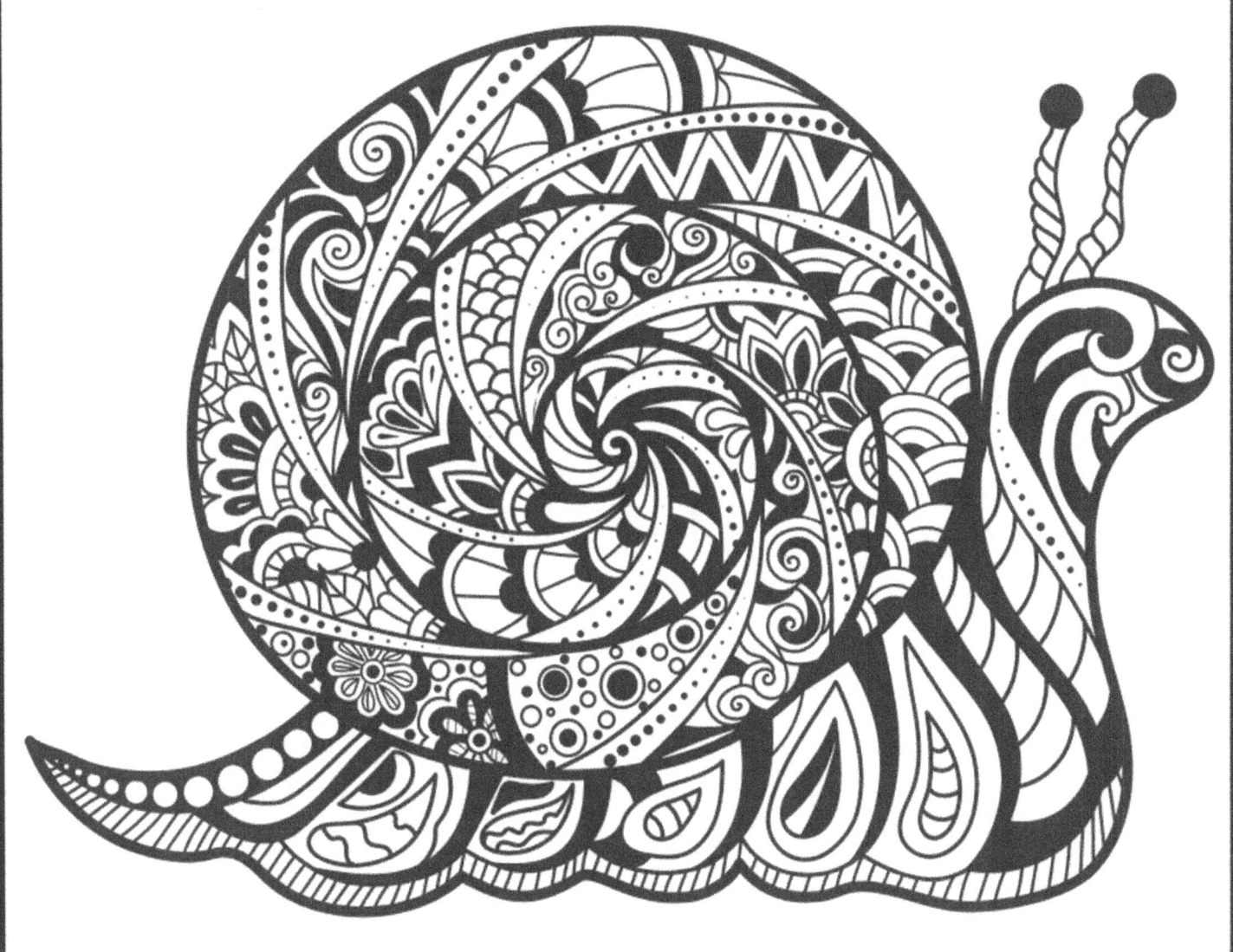

Color This Snail

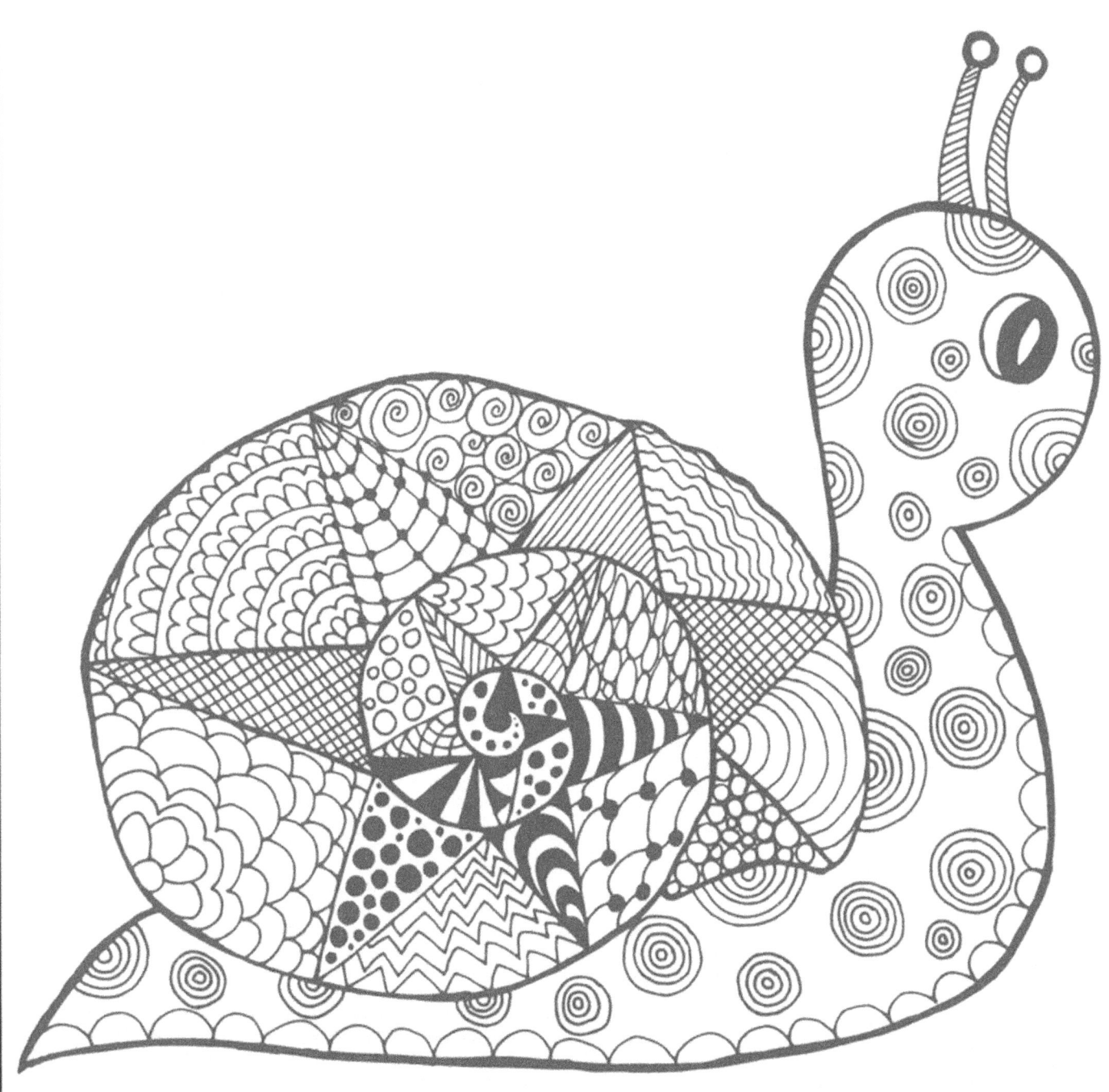

Color This Spot!

Color This Snail

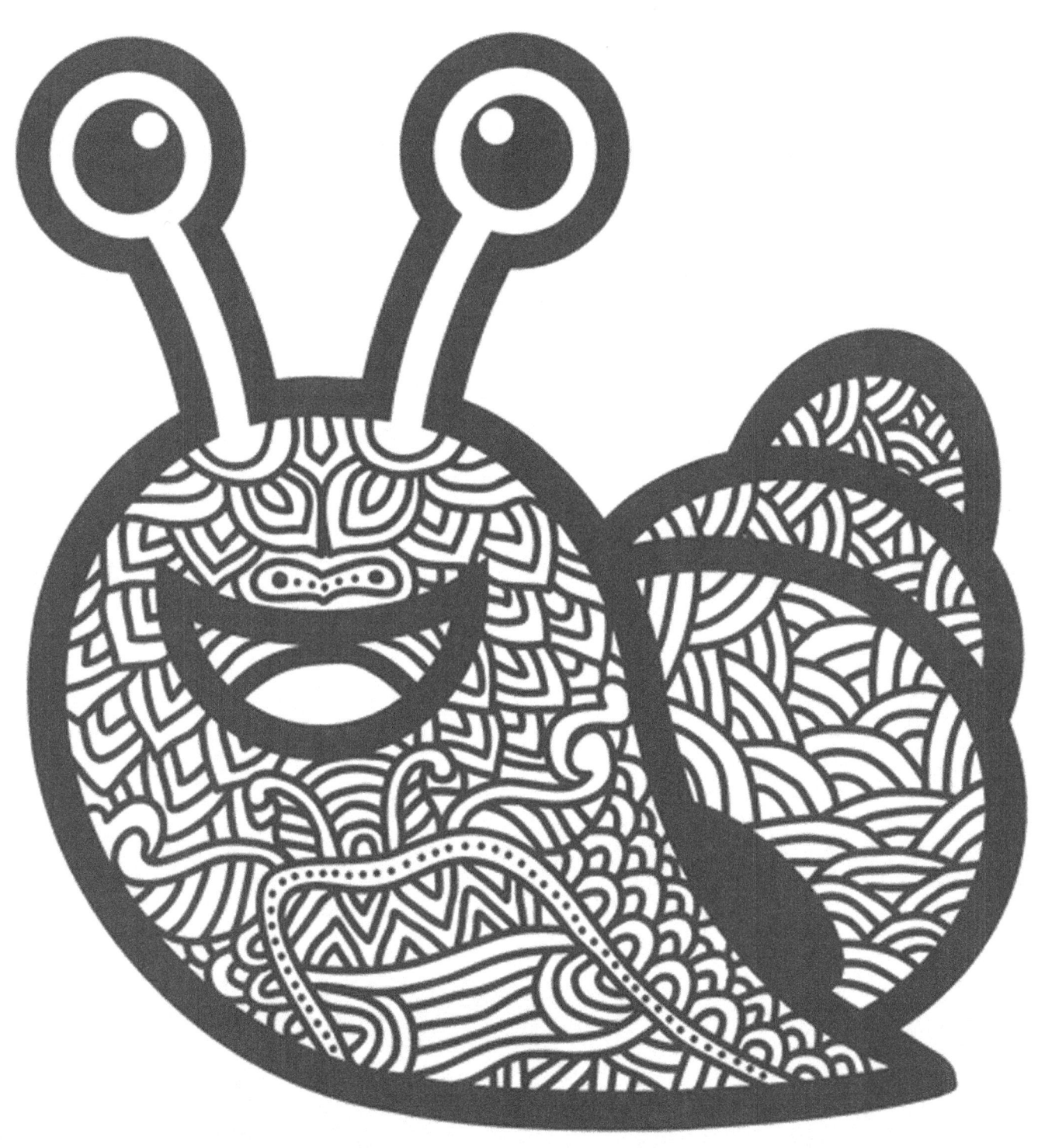

Color This small

Color This Snail

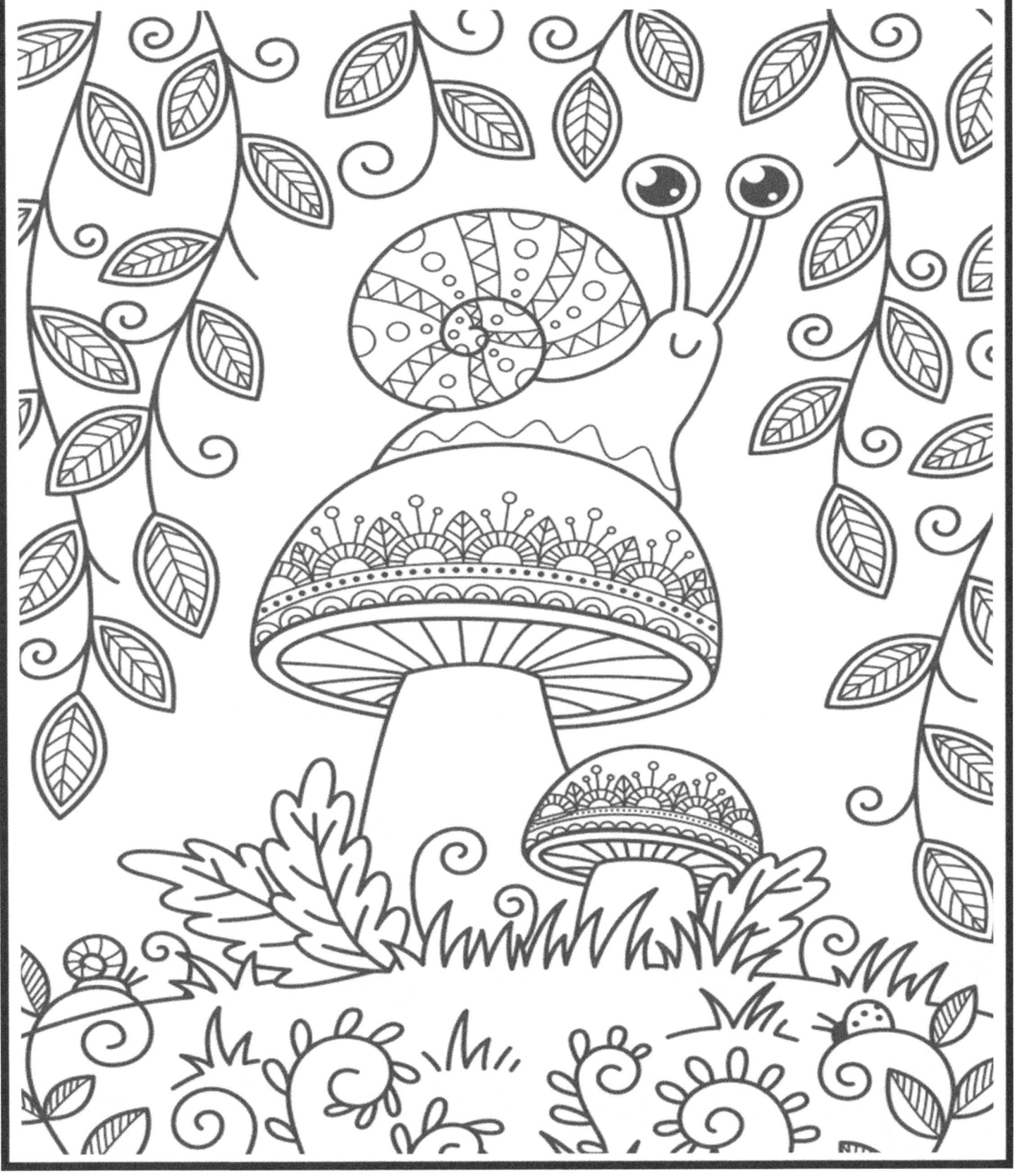

Color This Snail

Color This Snail

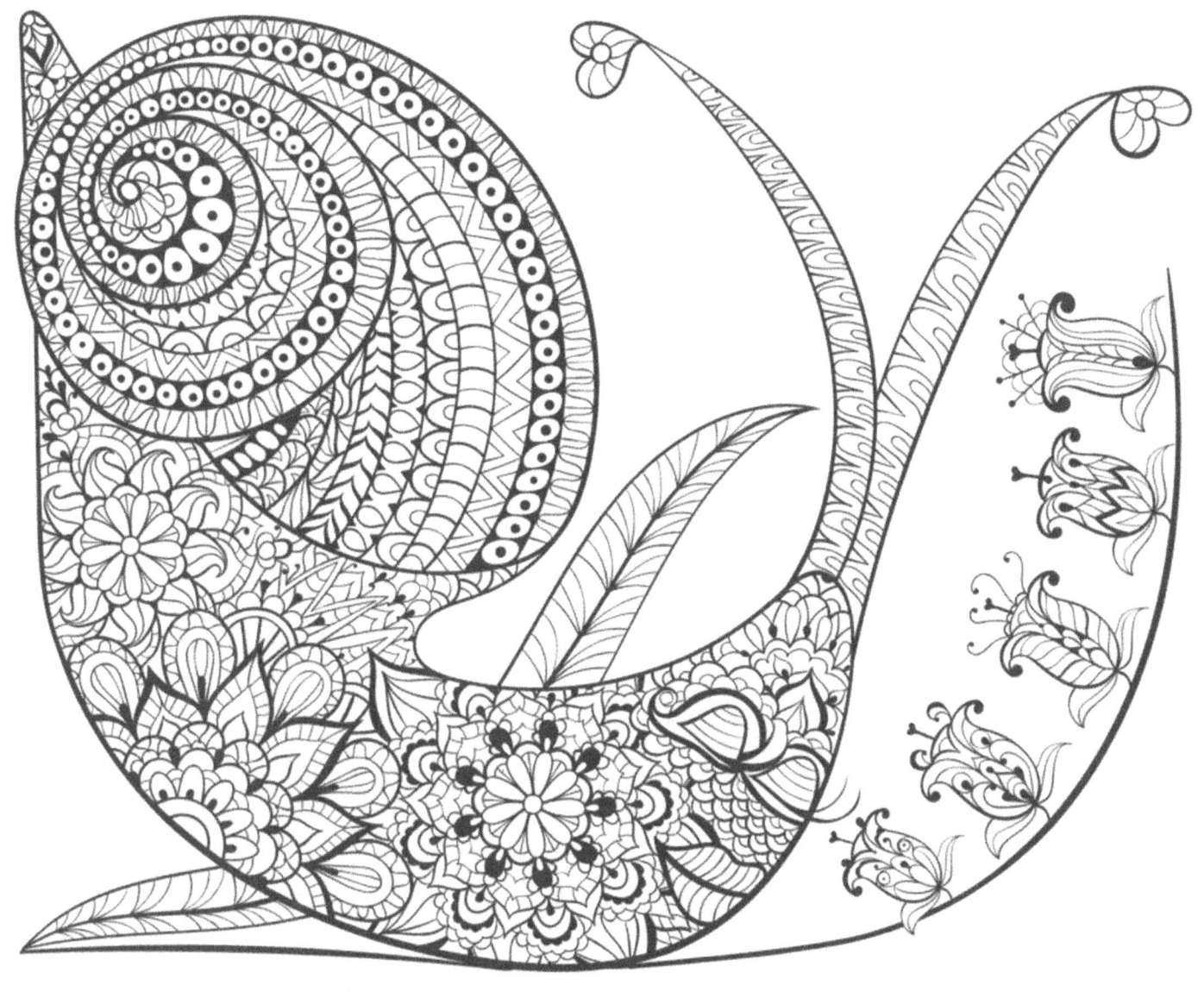

Color This Seal

Color This Snail

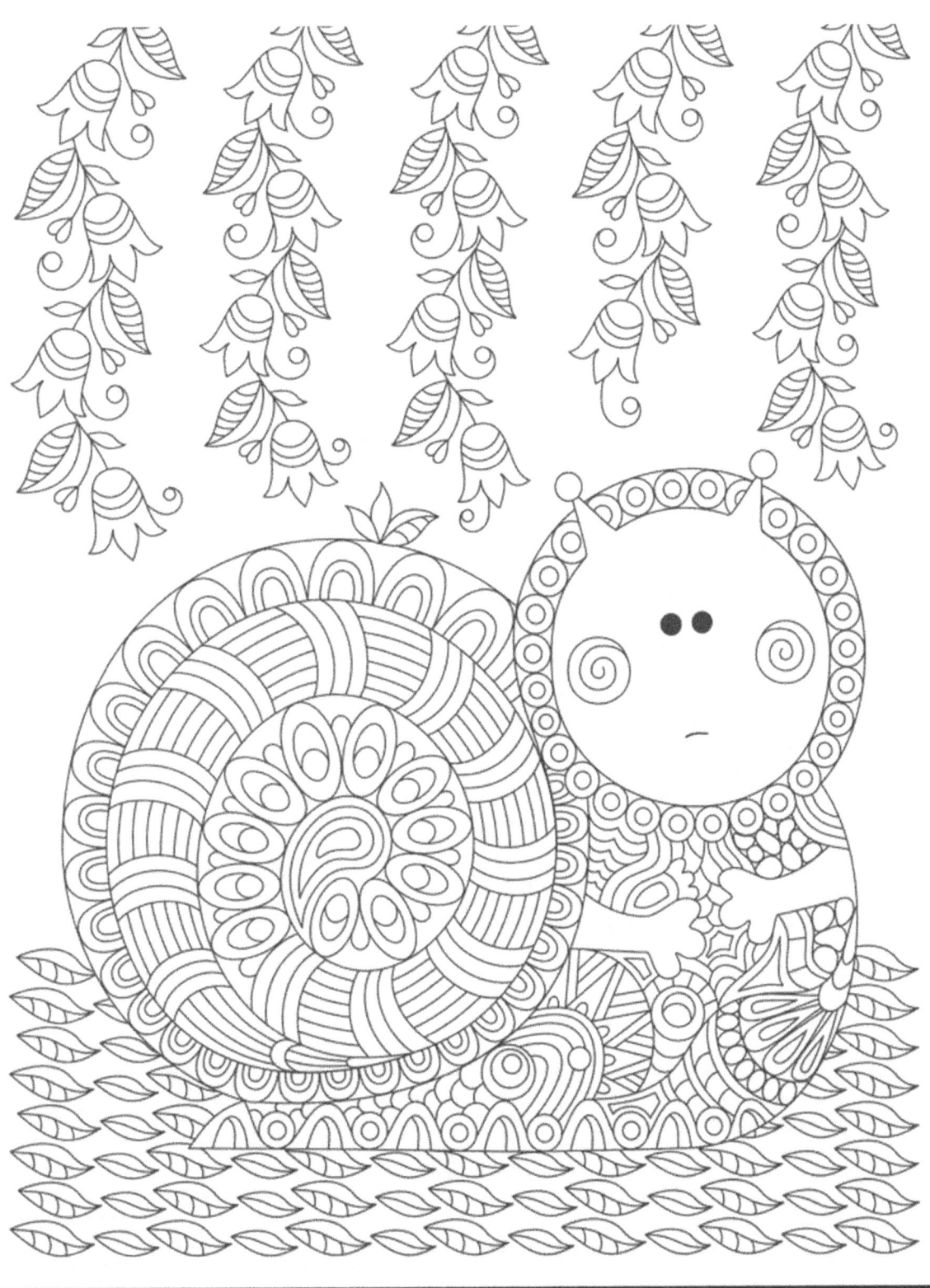

Color This Snail

Color This Snail

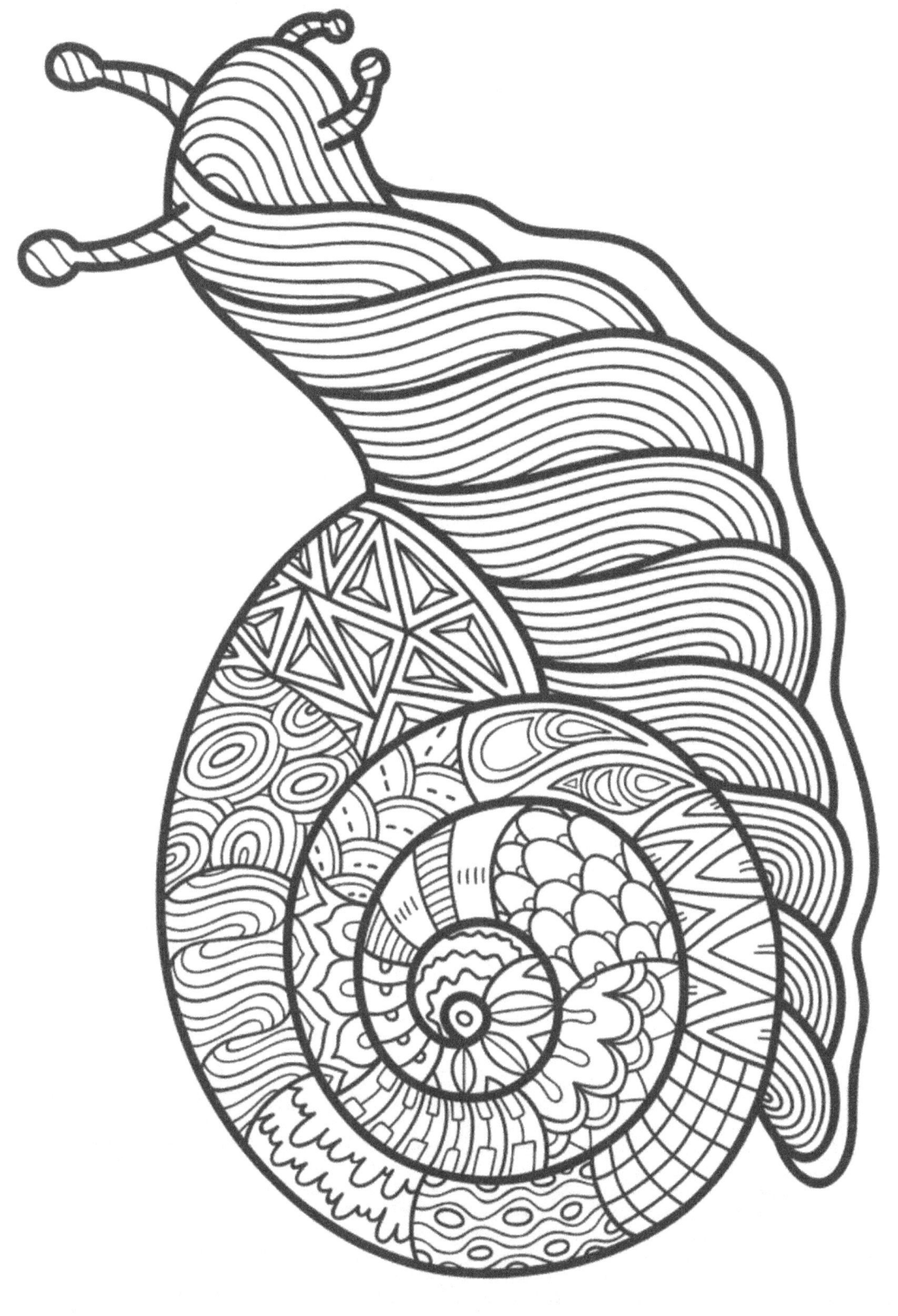

Color This Snail

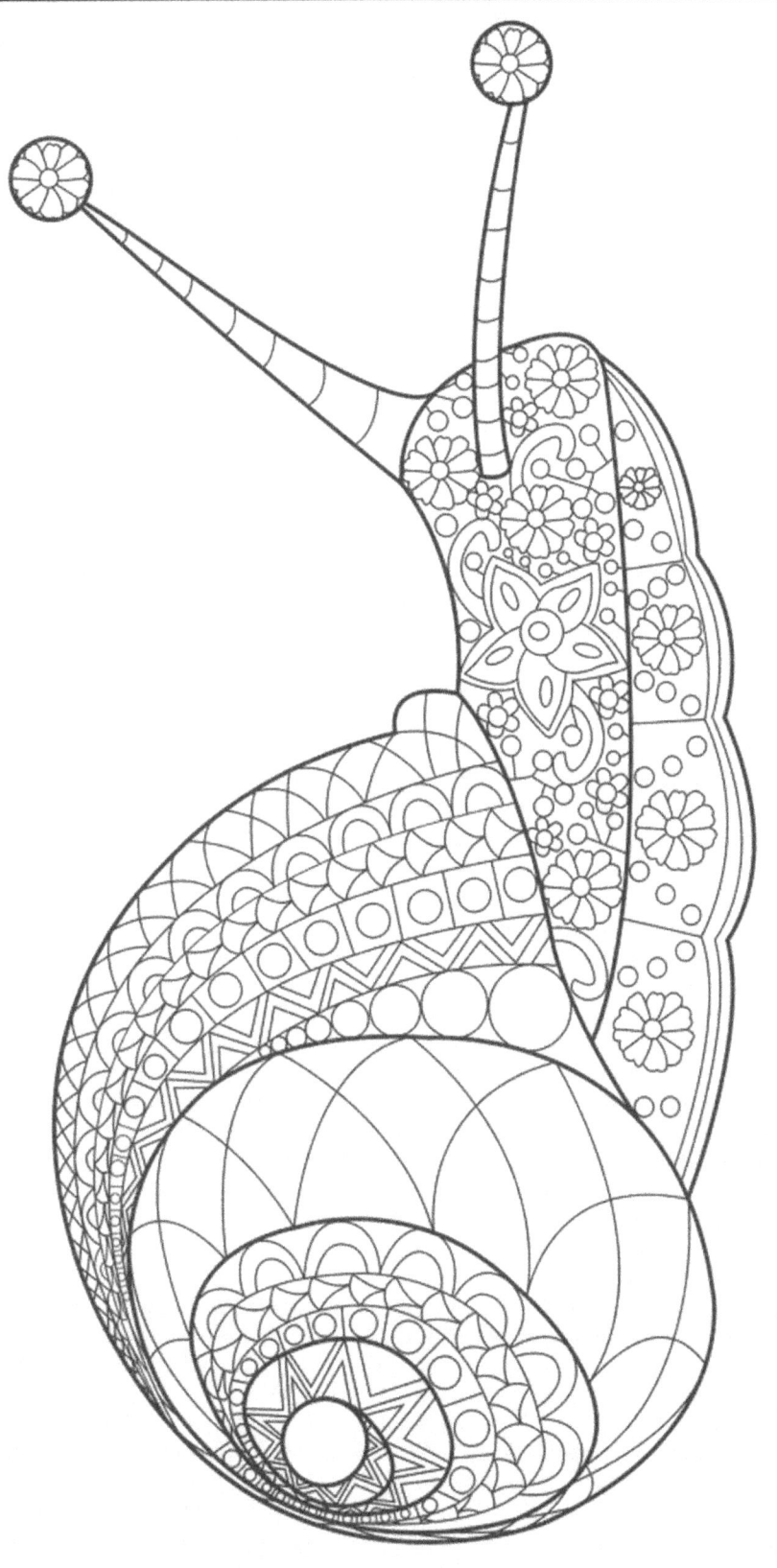

Color This Snail

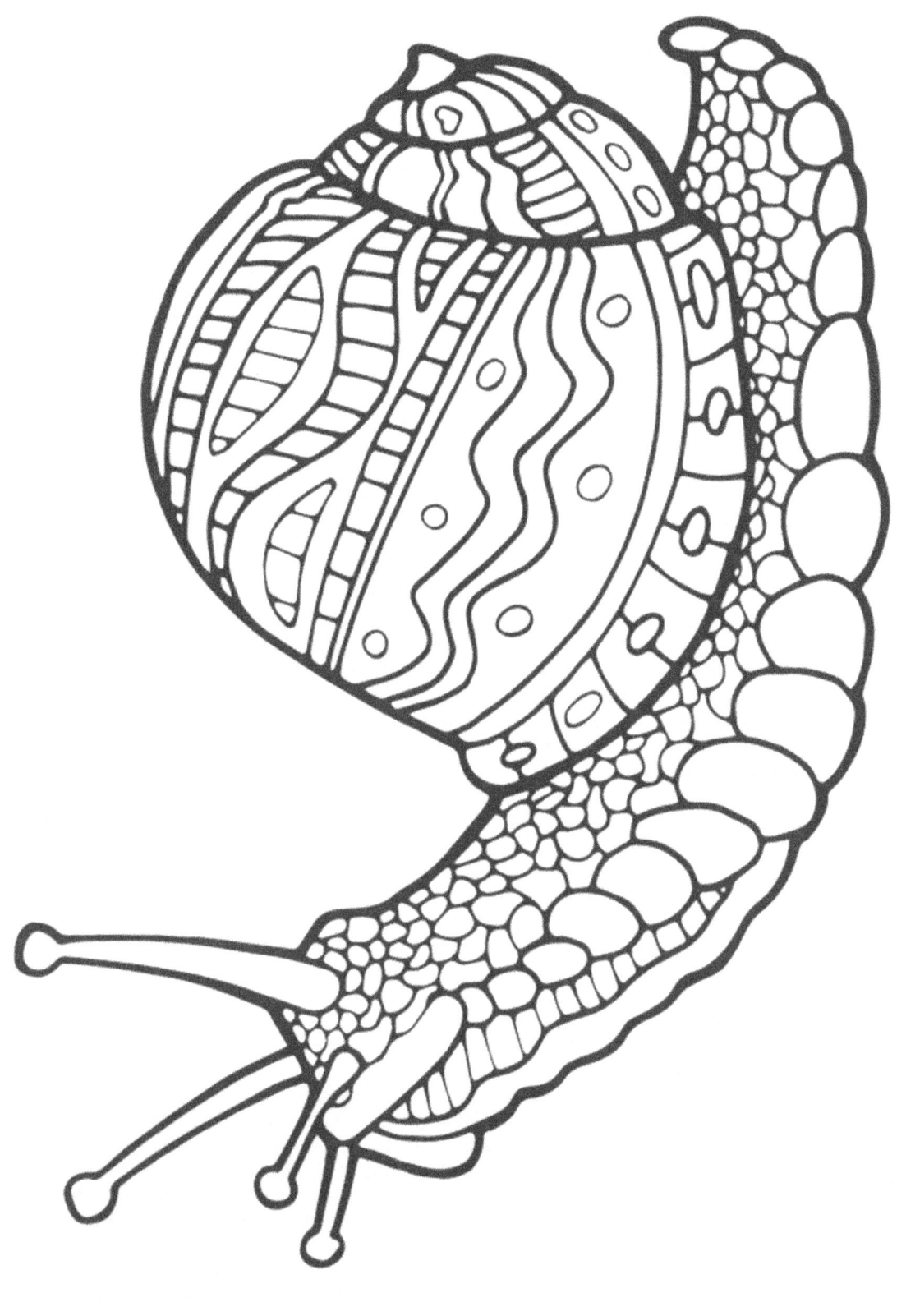

Color This Snail

Color This Snail

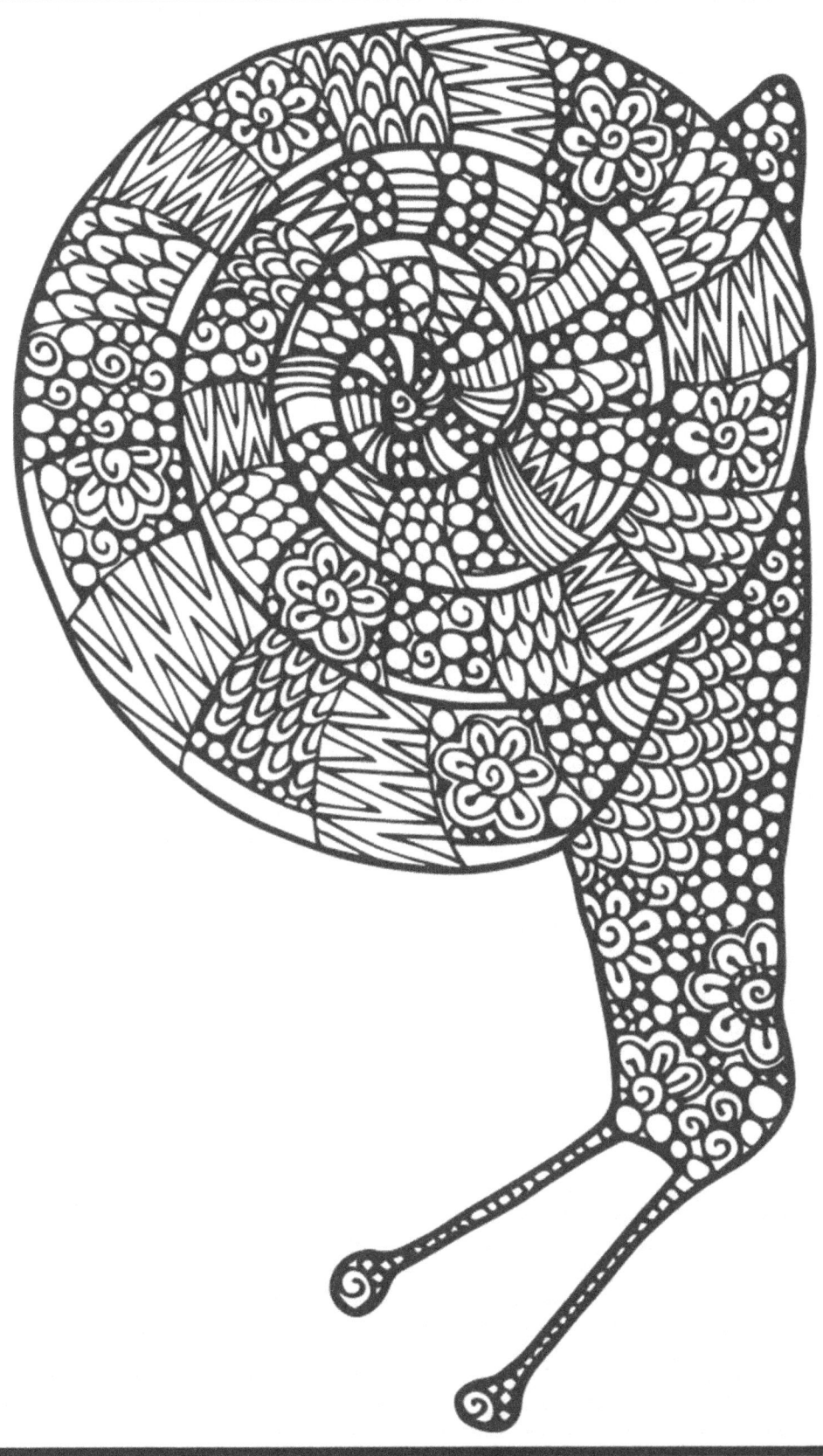

Color This Small

Color This Snail

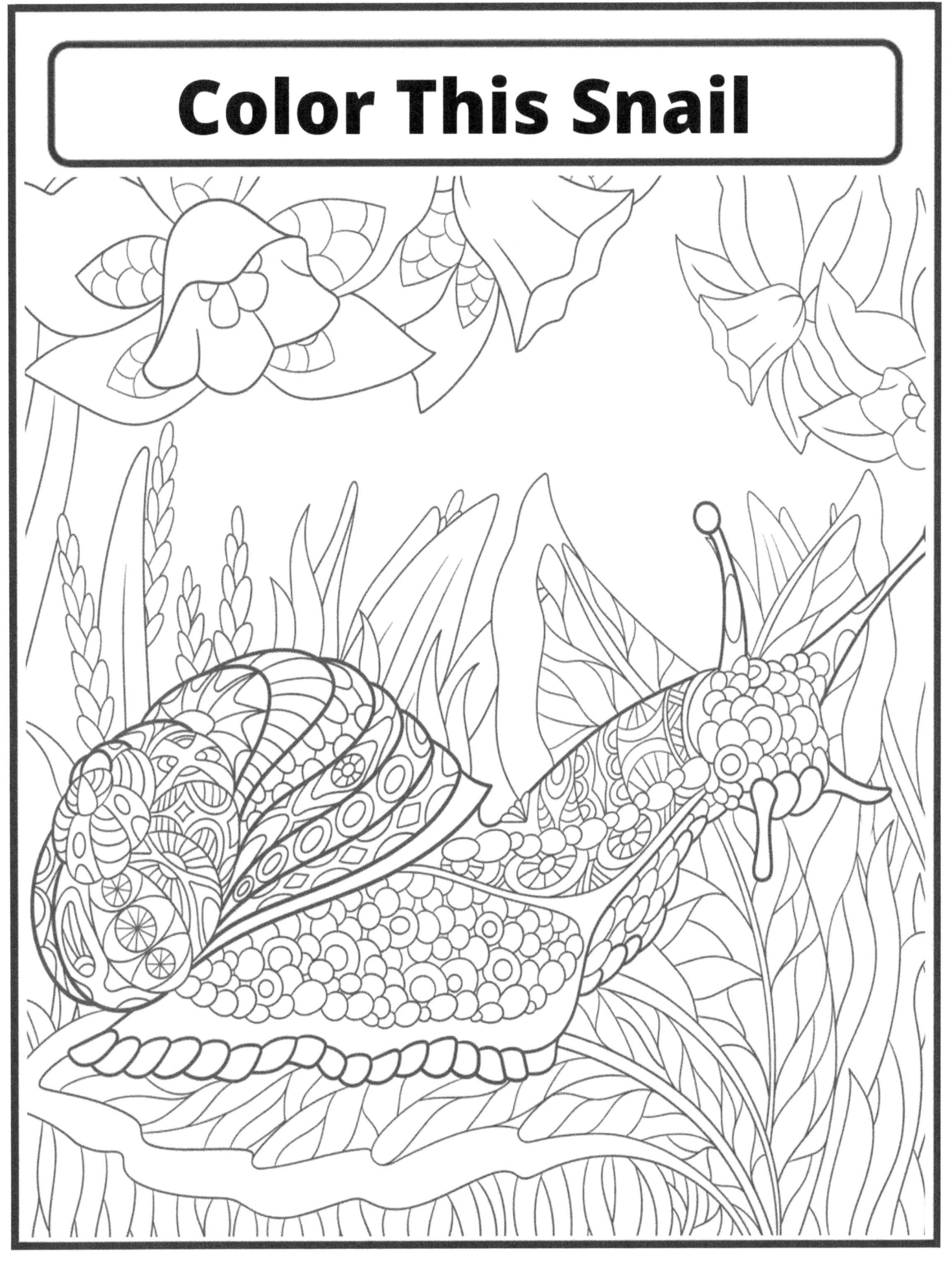

Color This Snail

Color This Snail

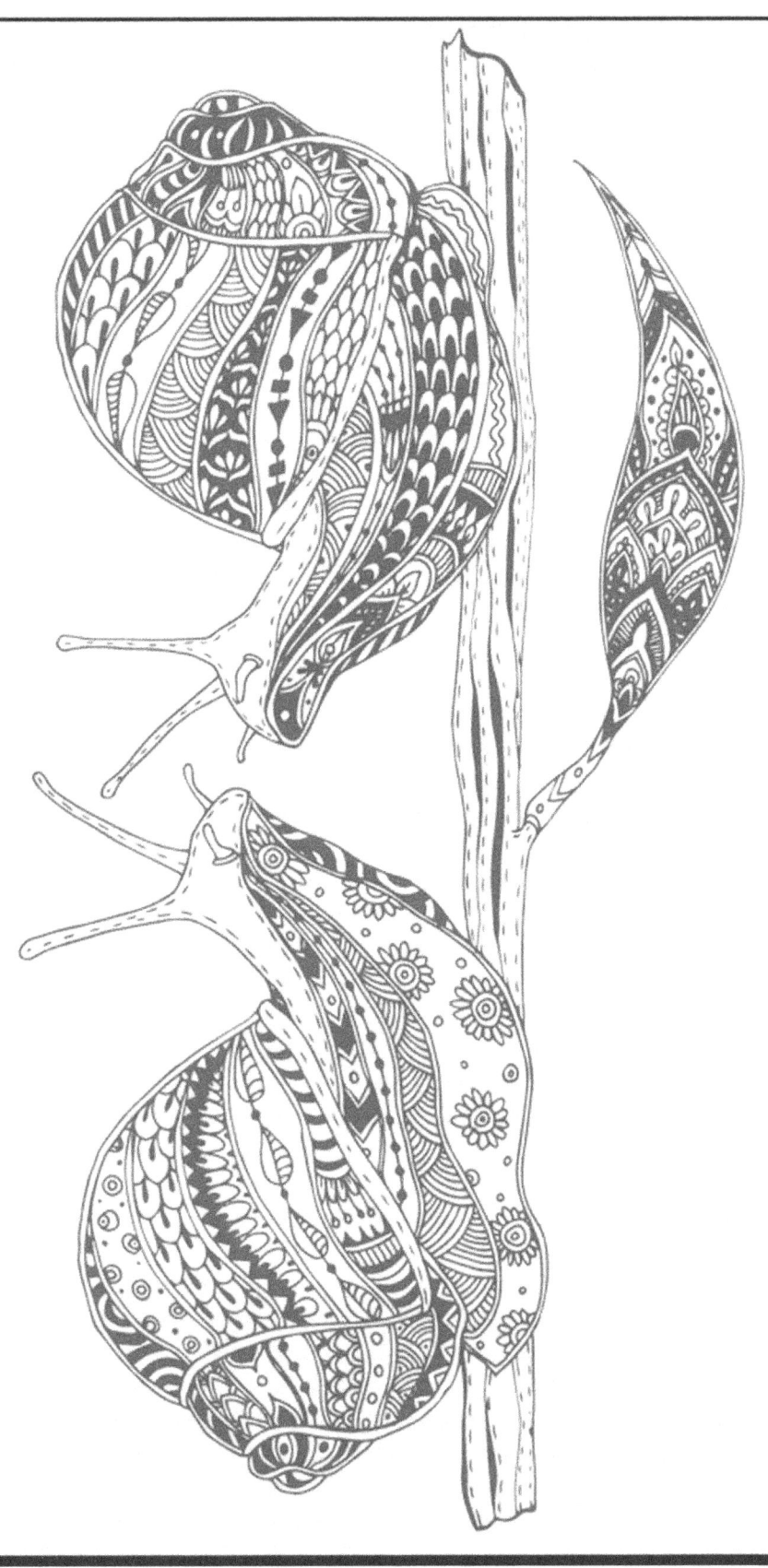

Color This Star!

Color This Snail

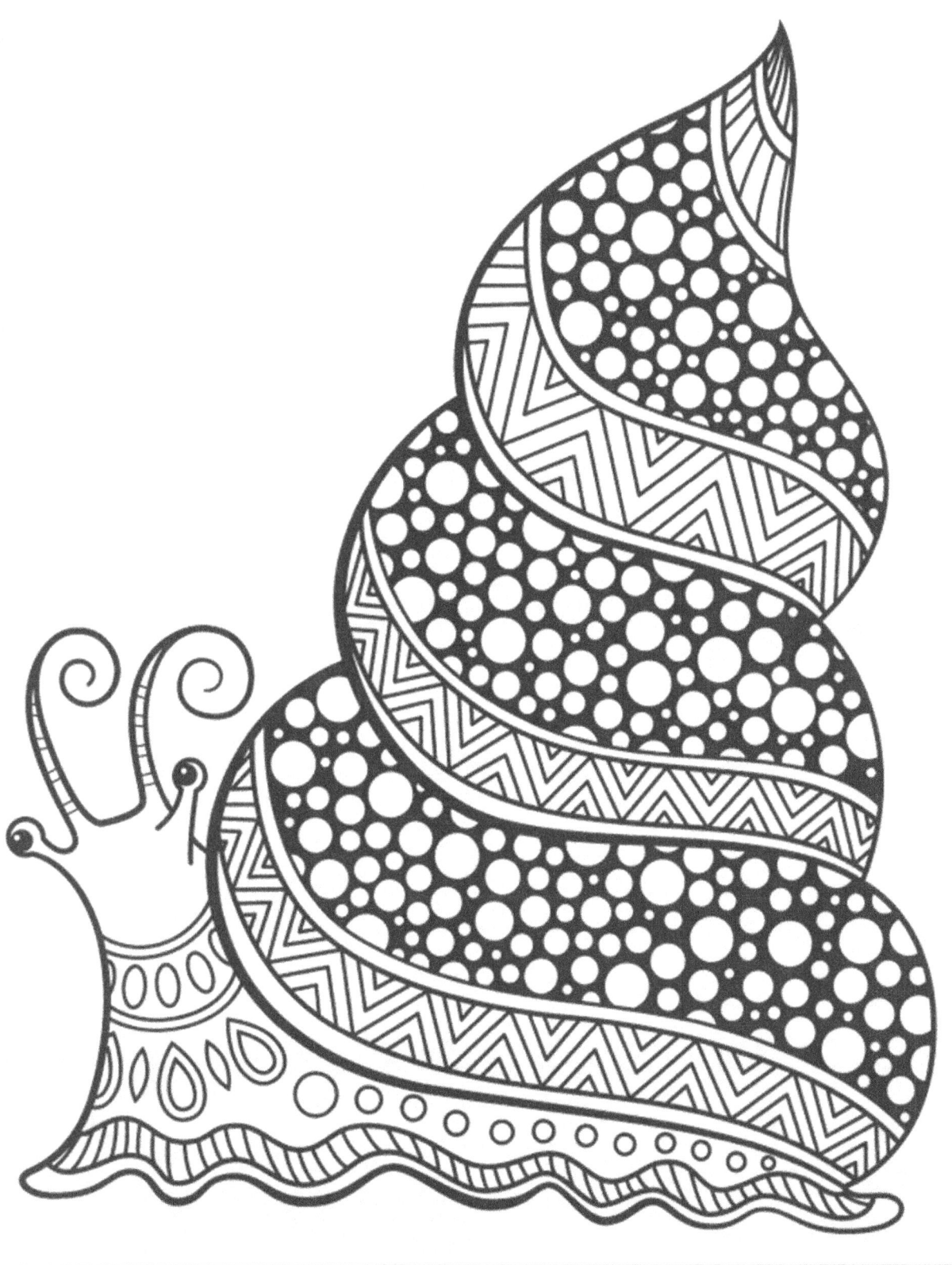

Color This Seal

Color This Snail

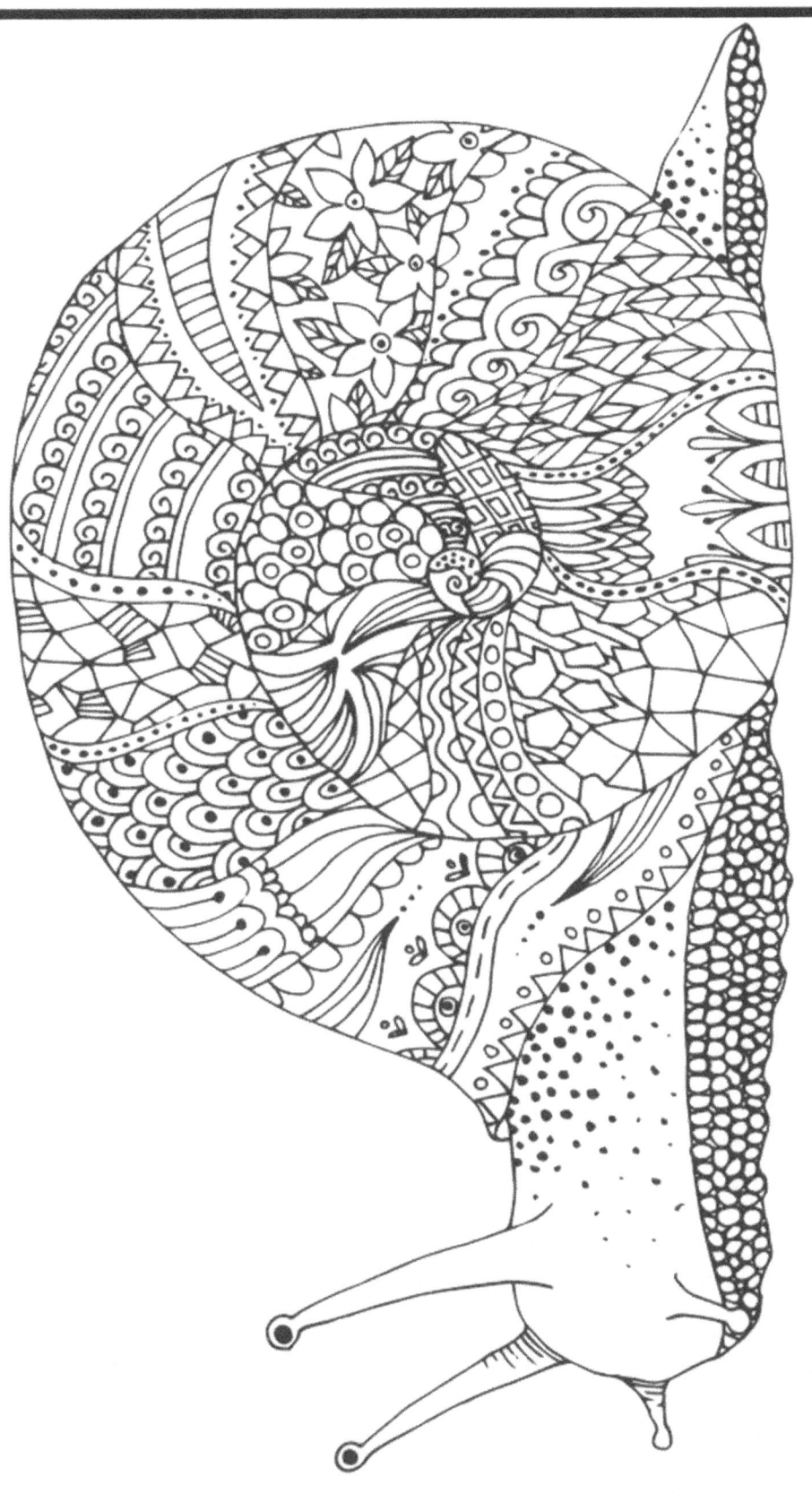

Color This Snail

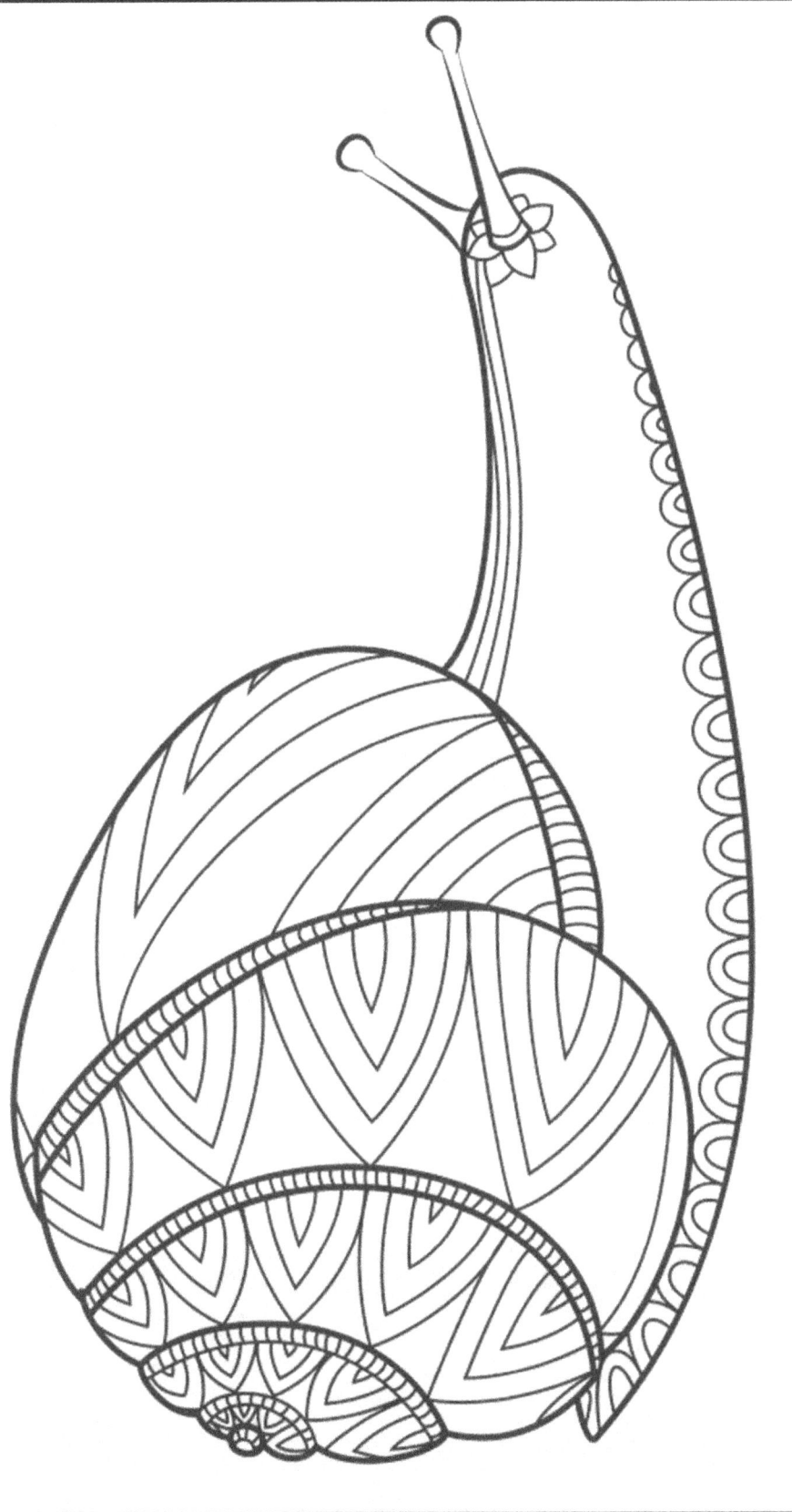

Color This Snail

Color This Snail

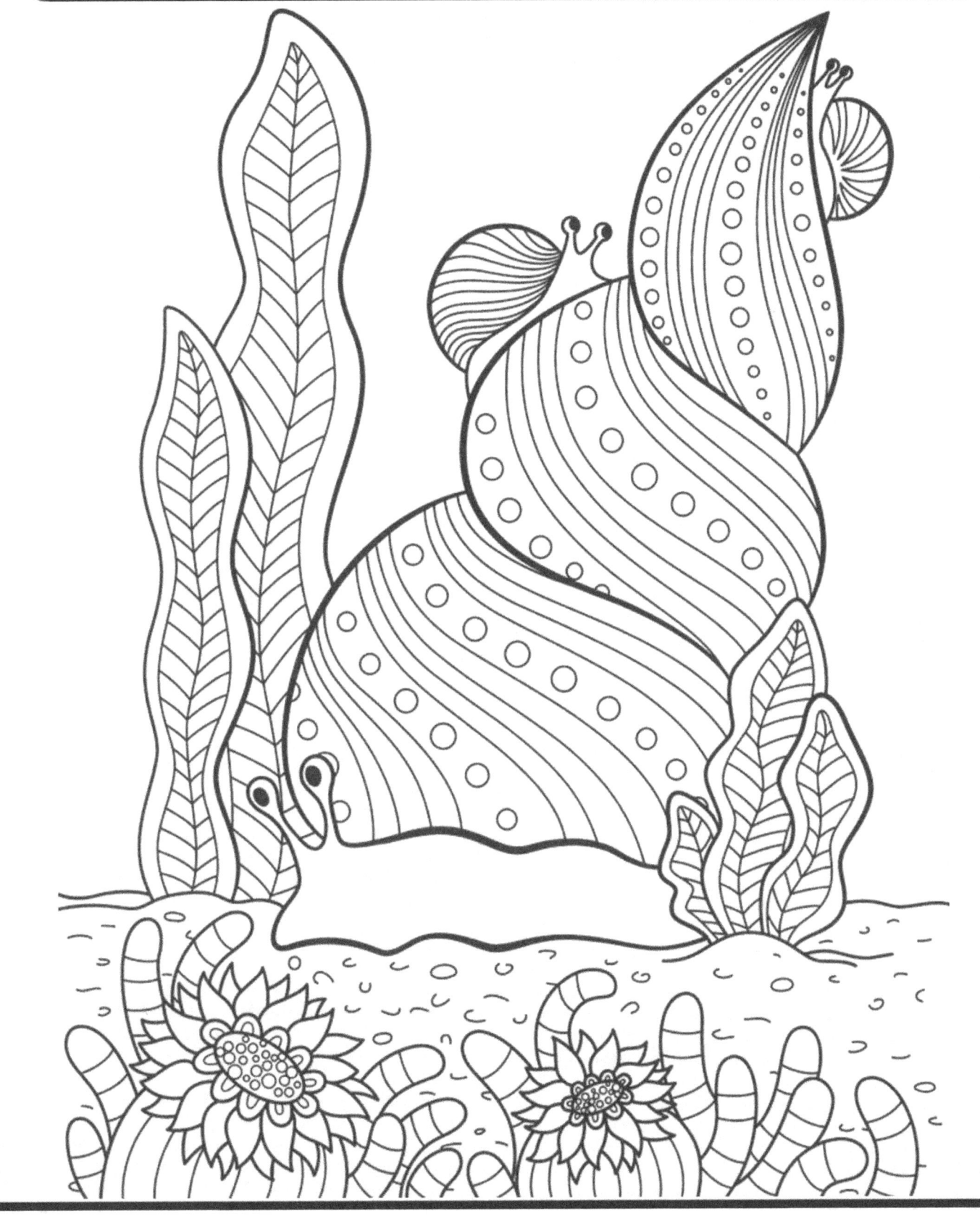

Color This Scroll

Color This Snail

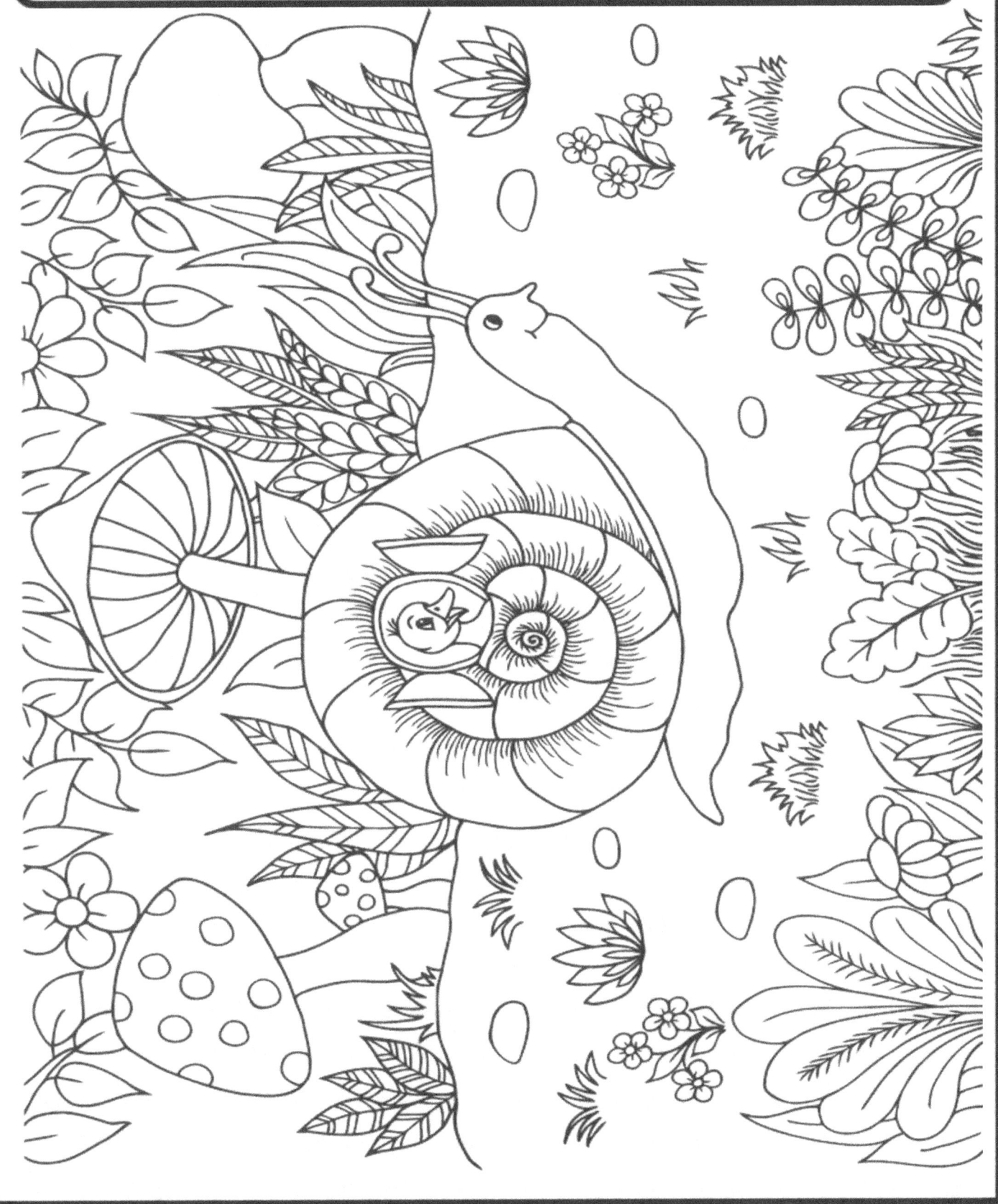

Color This Snail

Color This Snail

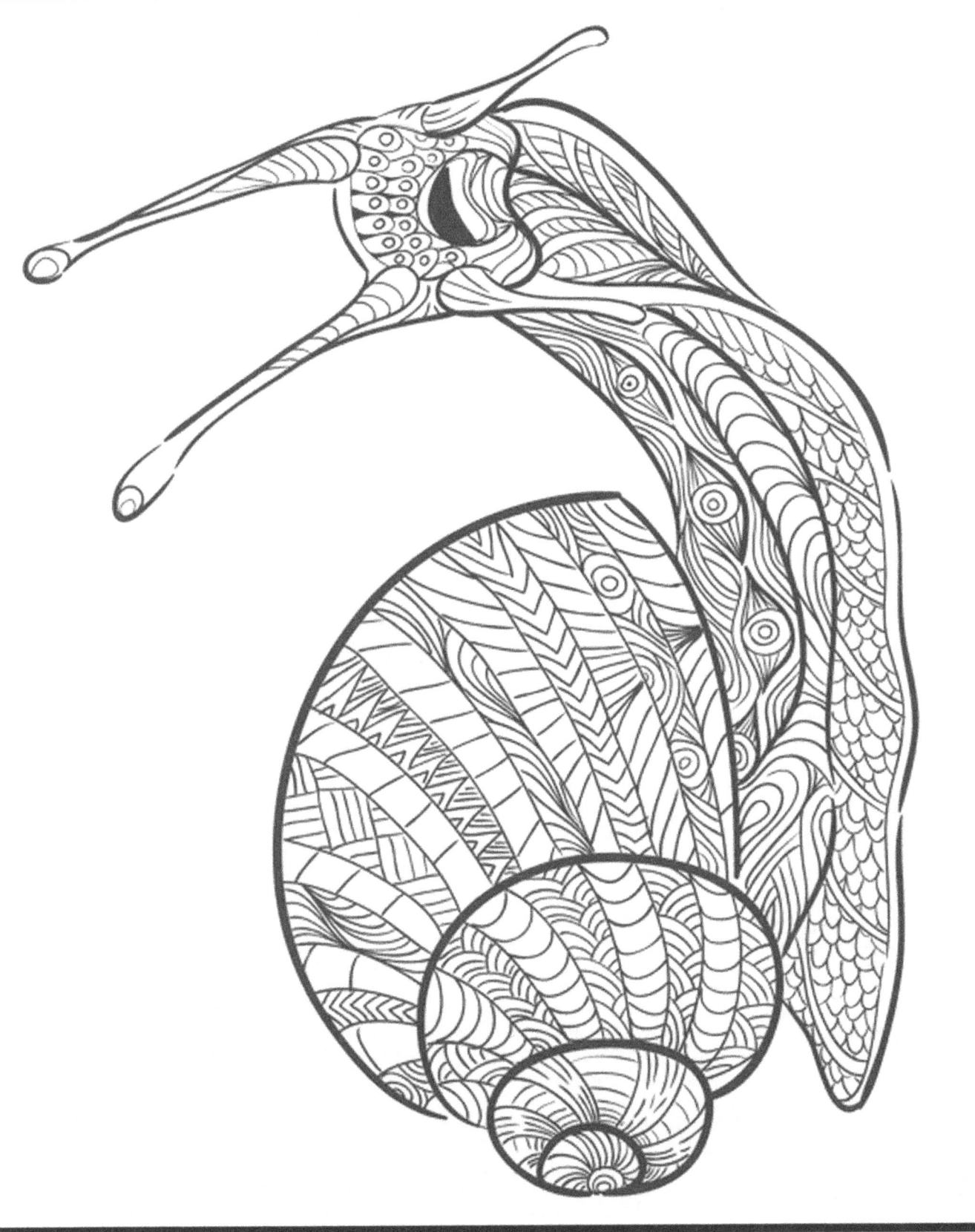

Color This Shelf

Color This Snail

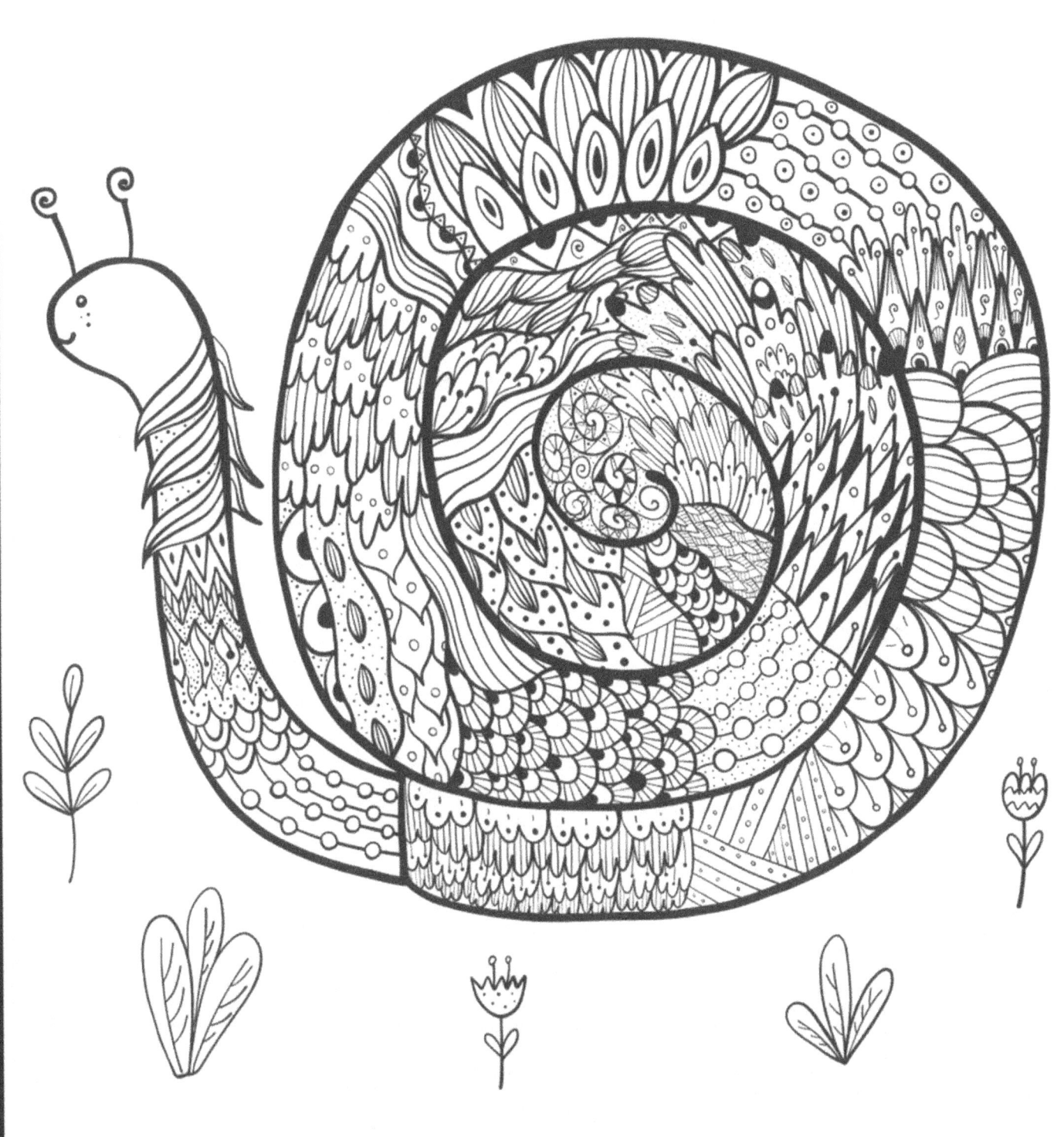

Color This Snail

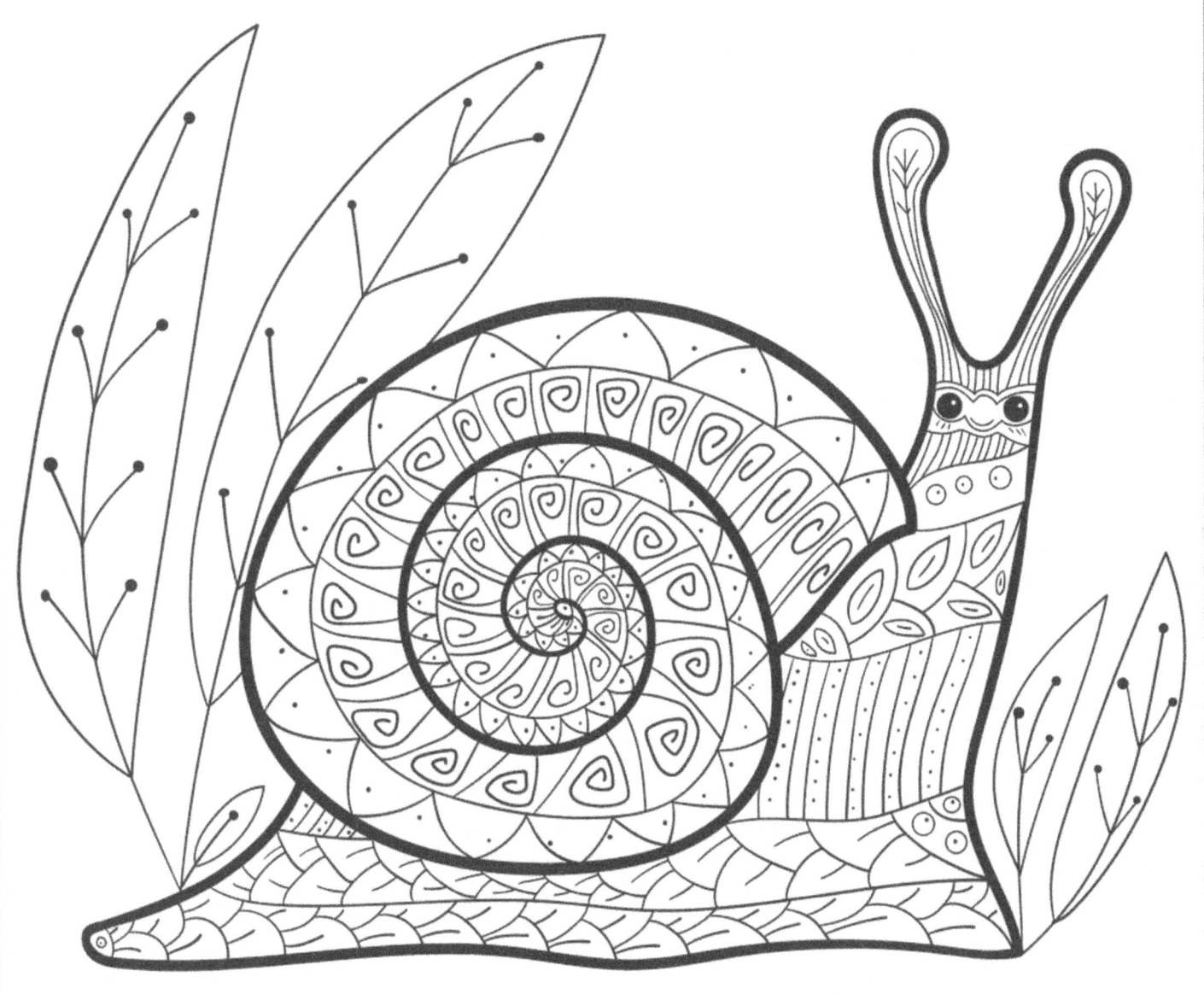

Color This Snail

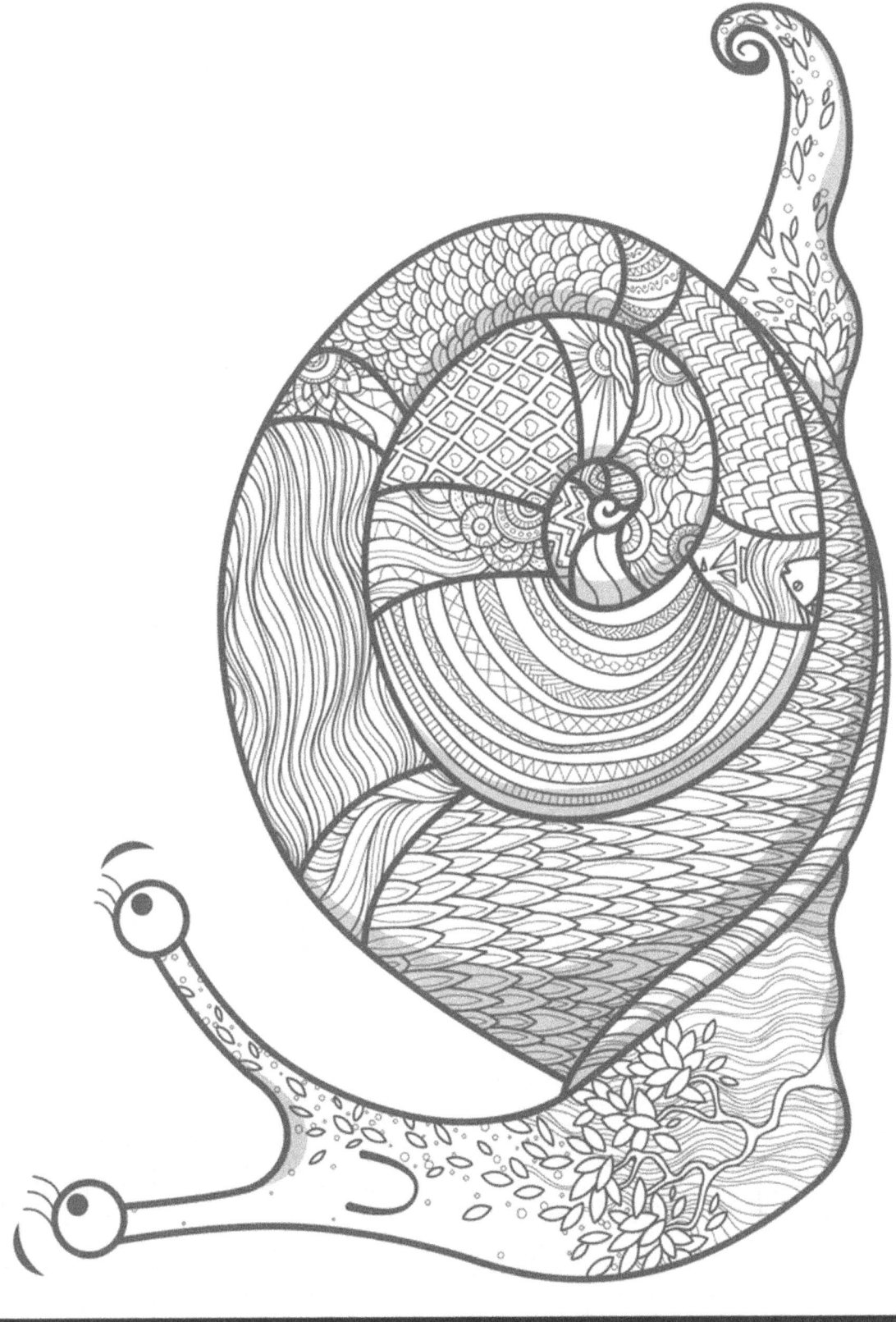

Color This Snail

Color This Snail

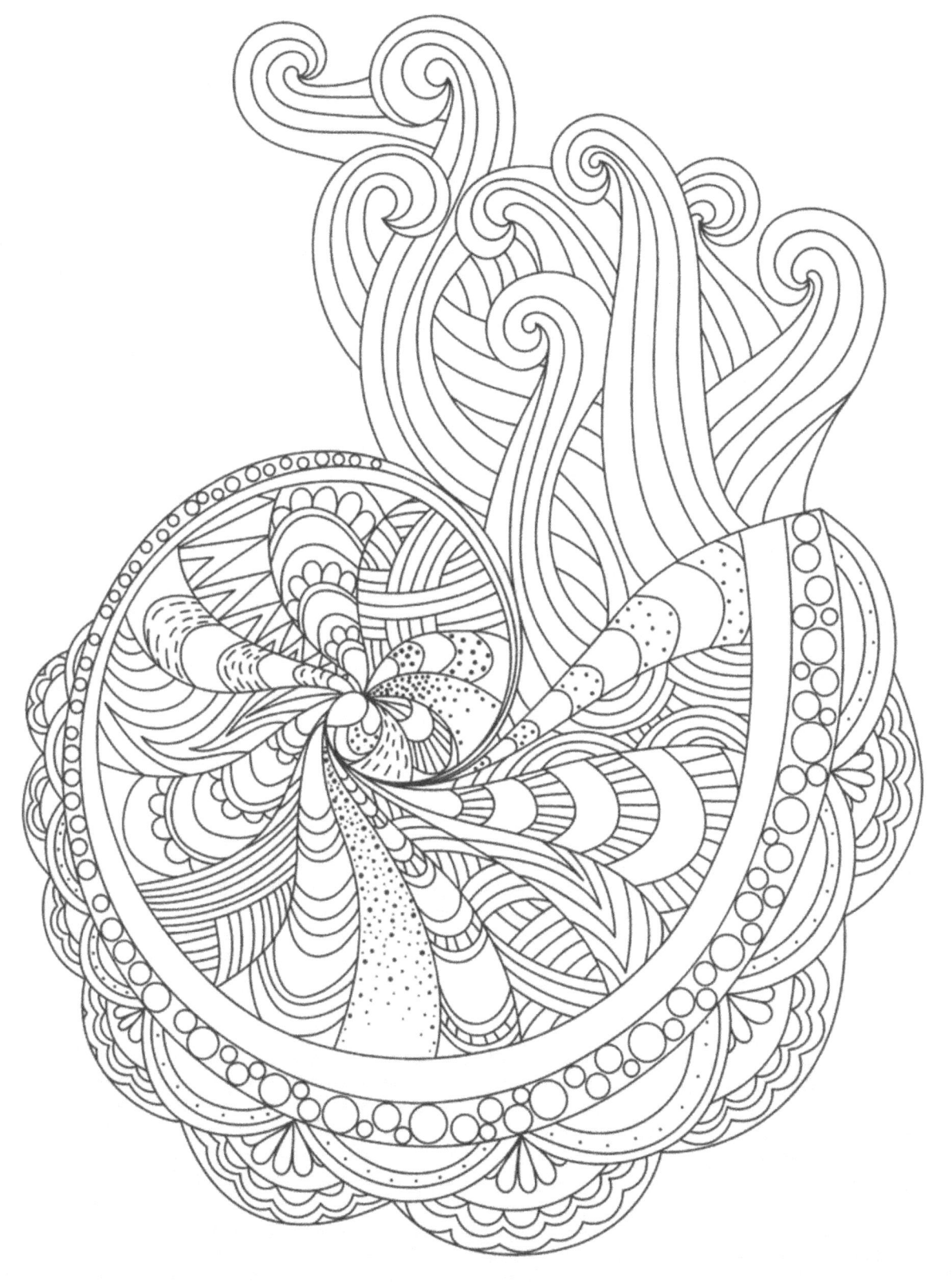

Color This Snail

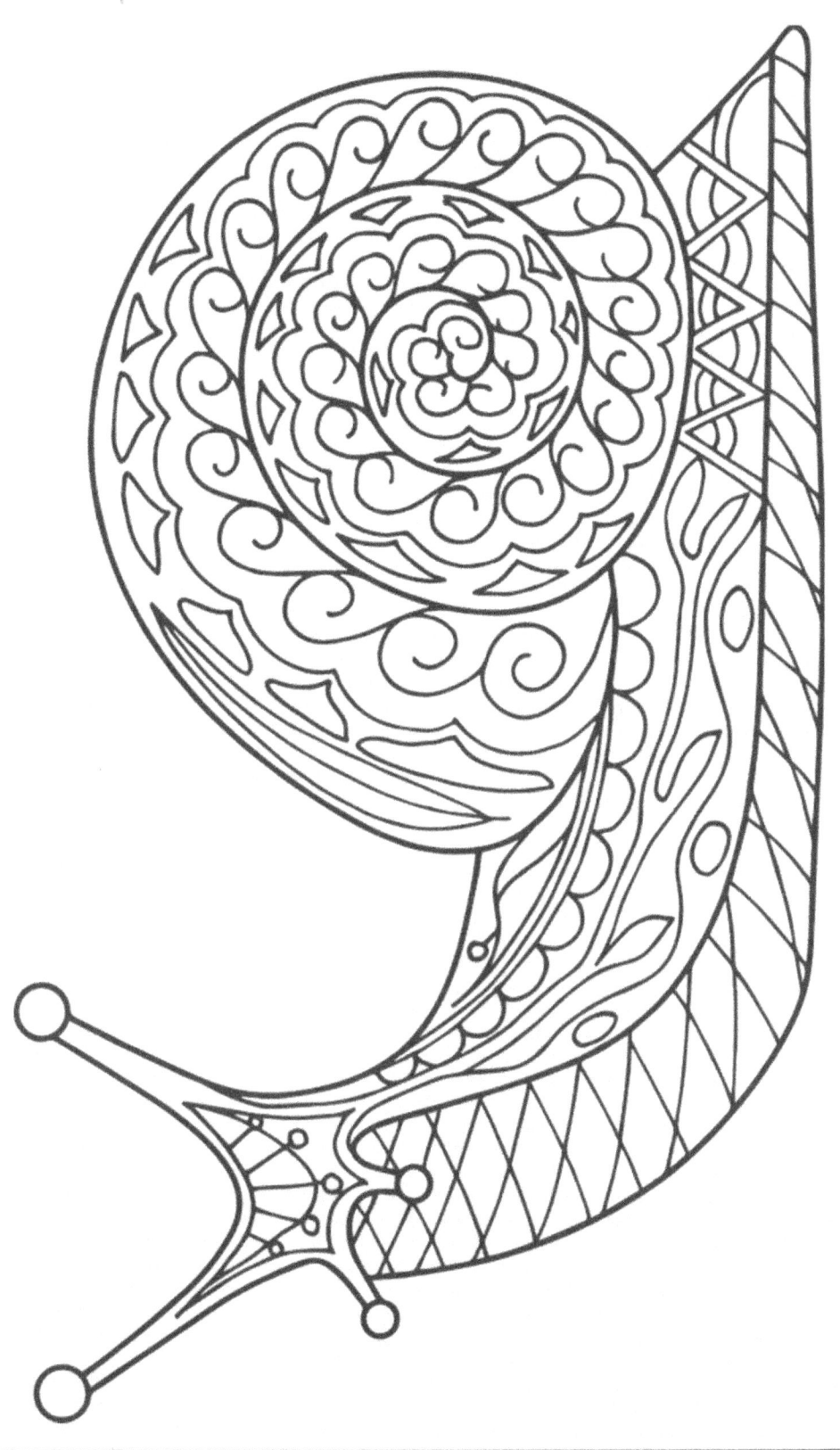

Color This Spell

Color This Snail

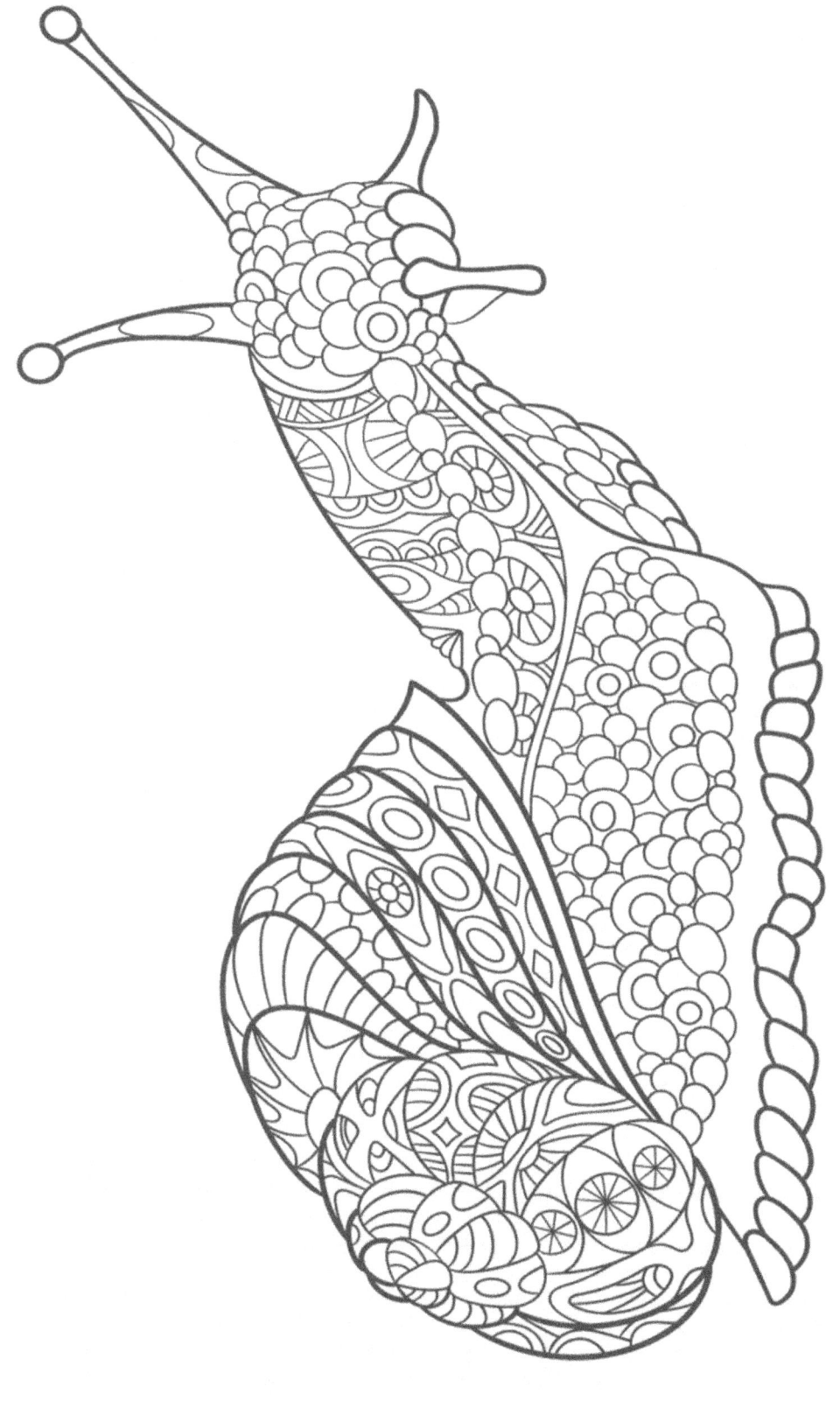

Color This Shell!

Color This Snail

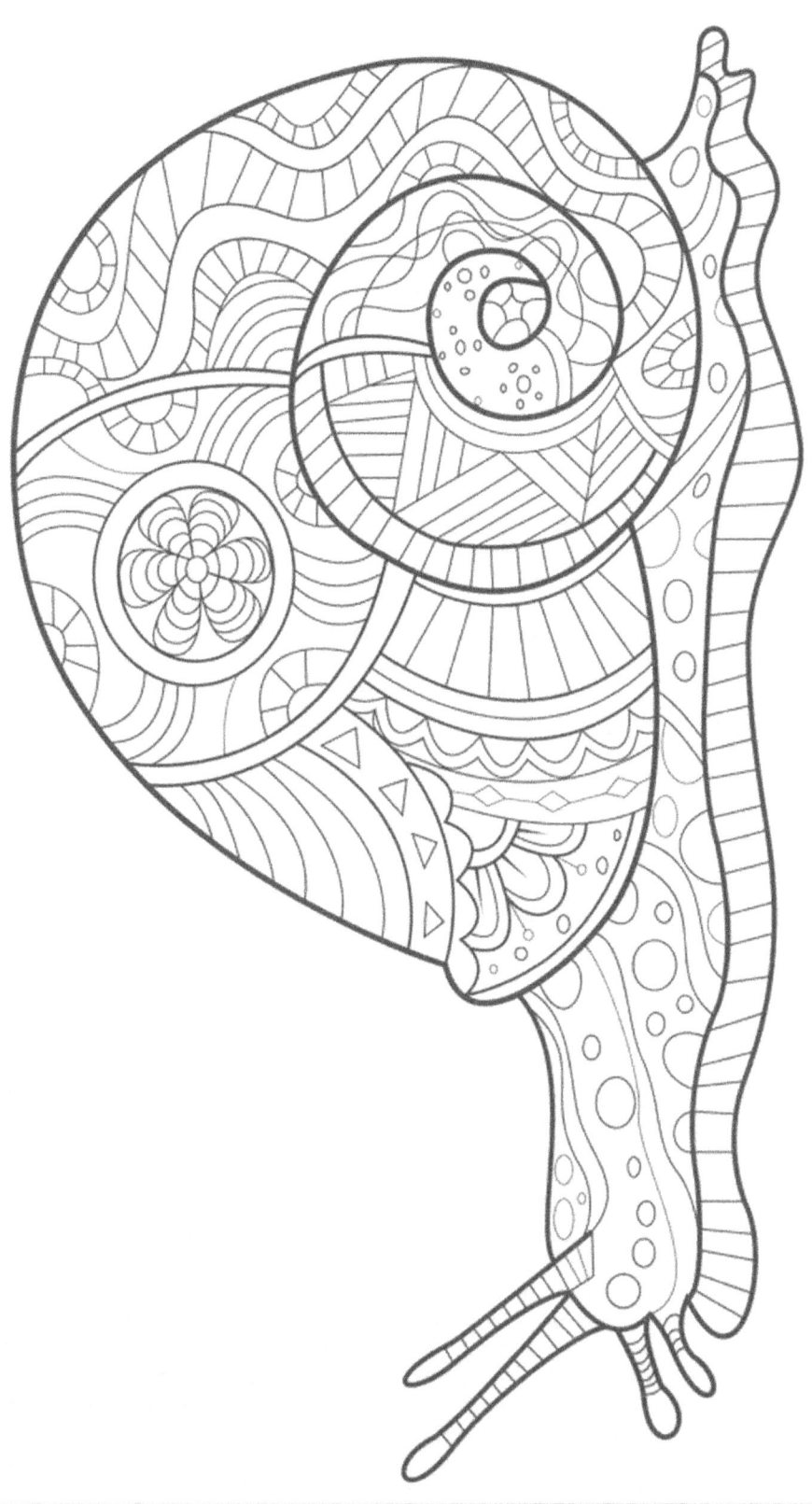

Color This Spell

Color This Snail

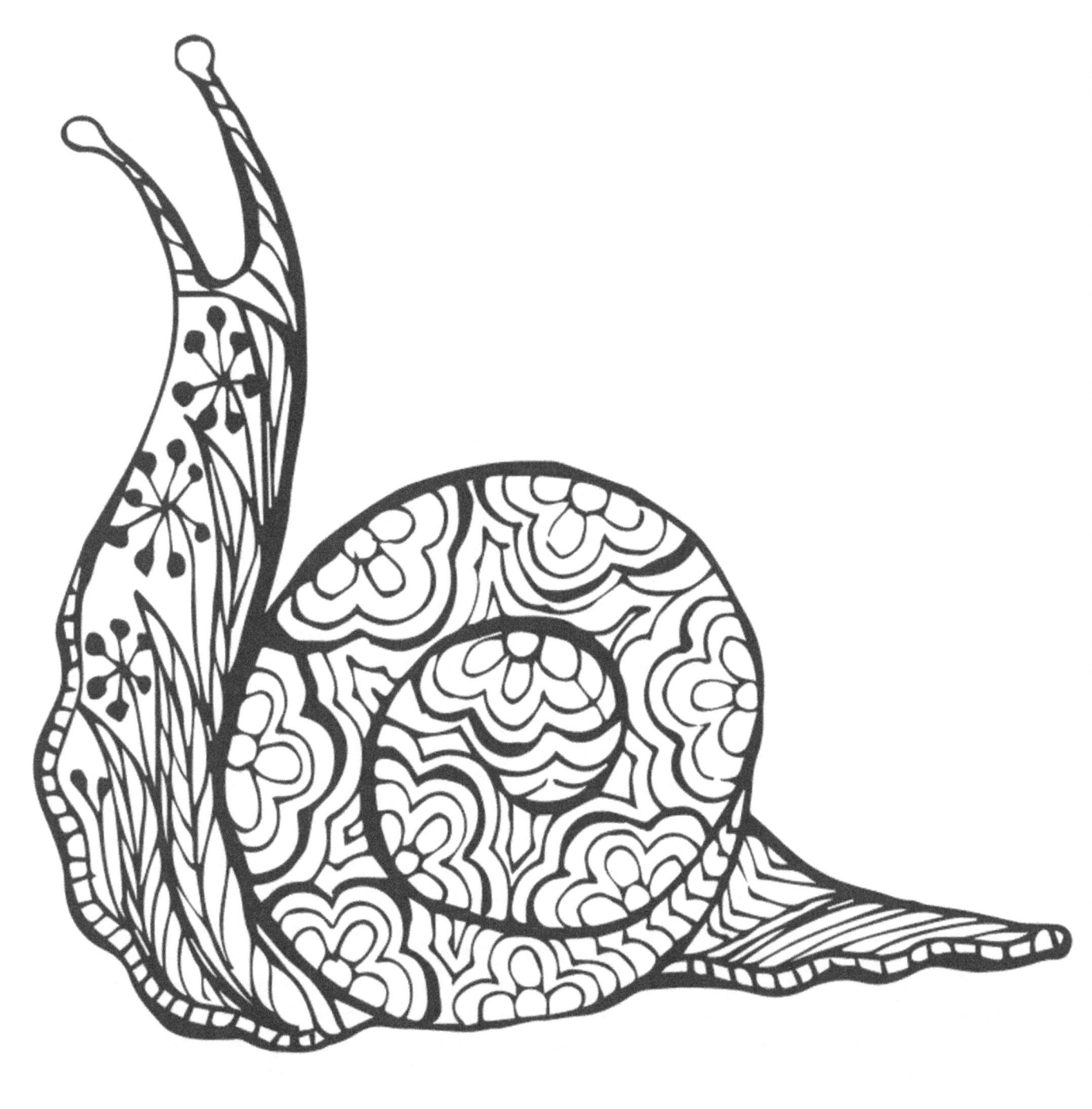

Color This Snail

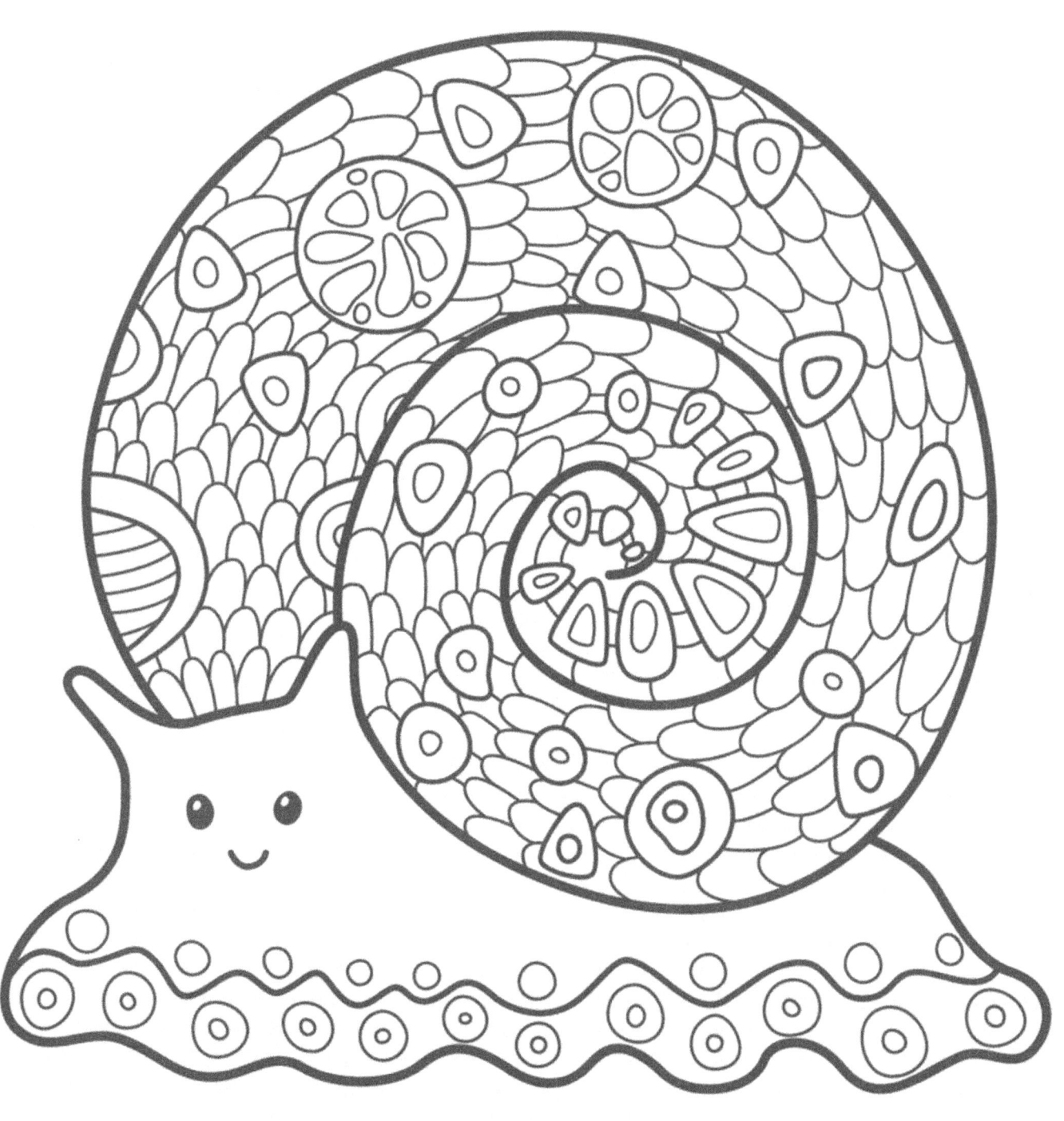

Color This Snail

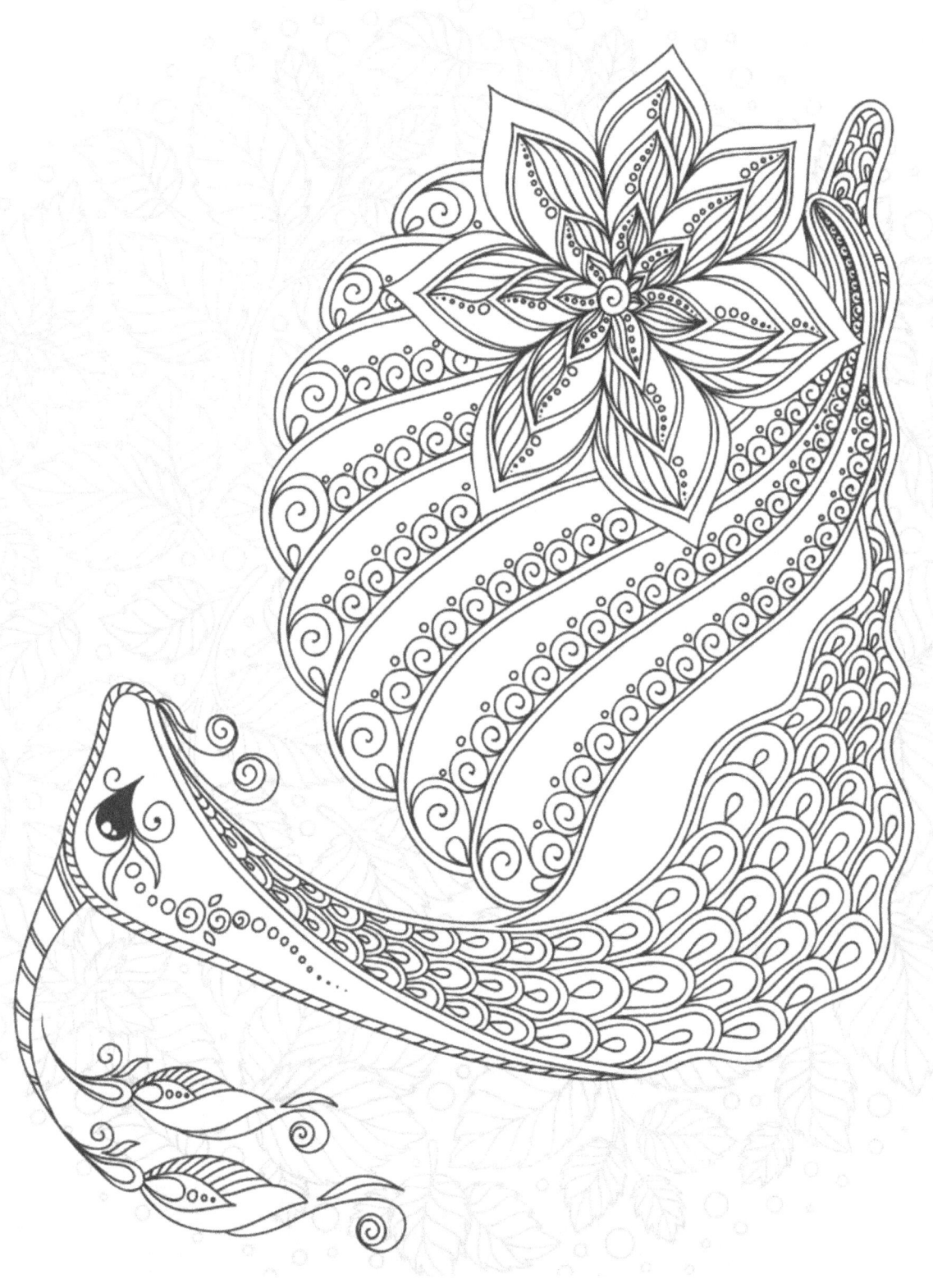

Color This Snail

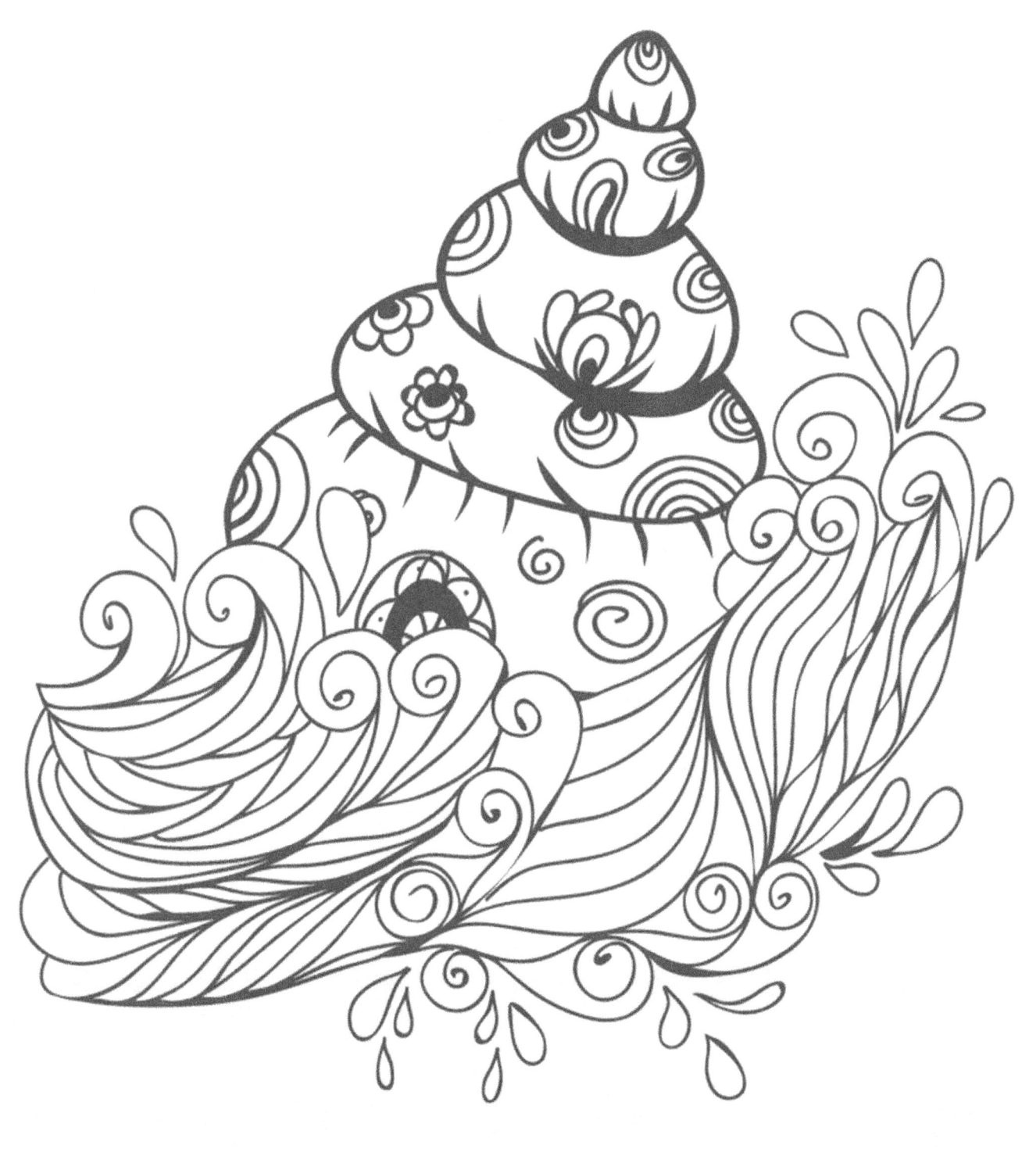

Color This Small

Color This Snail

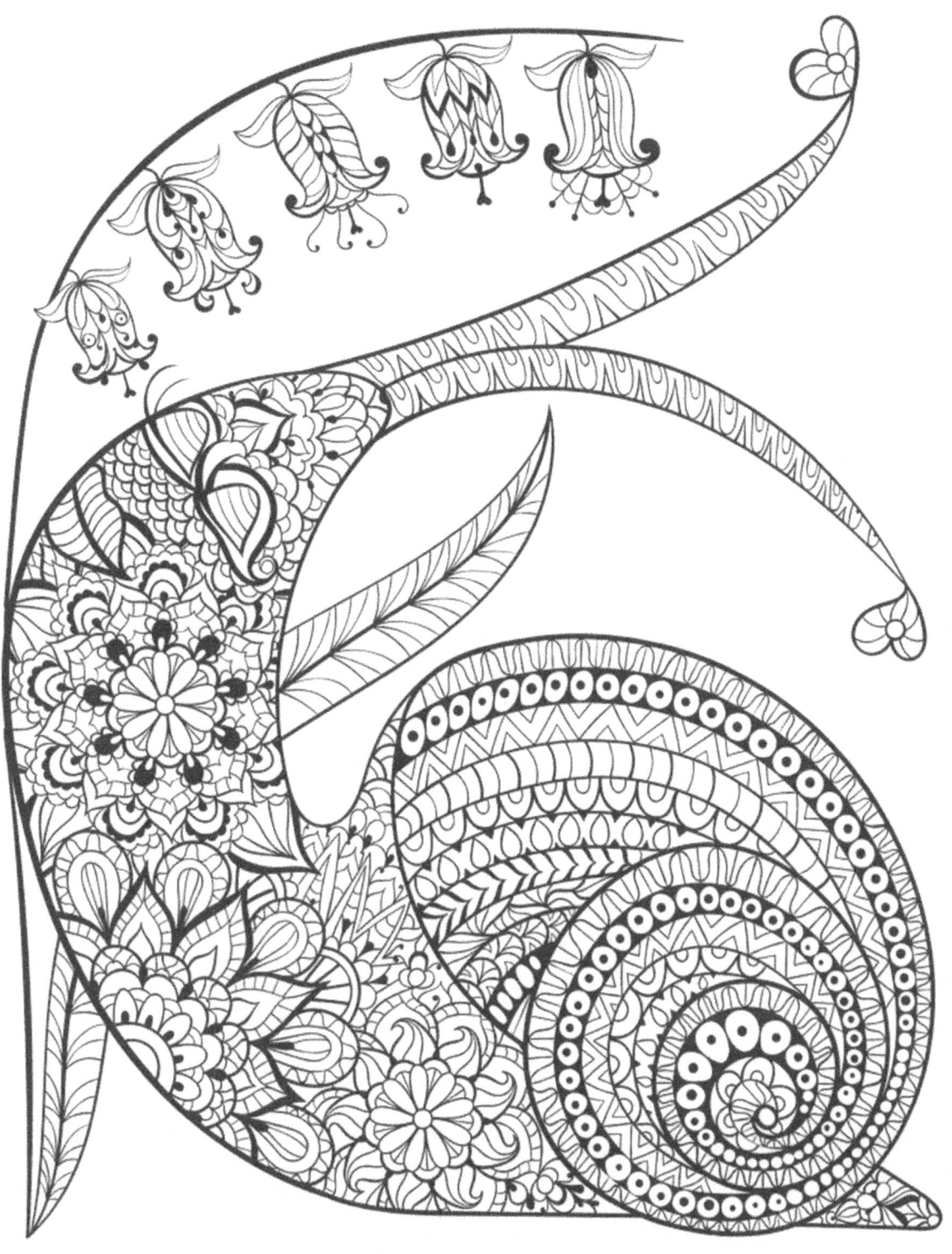

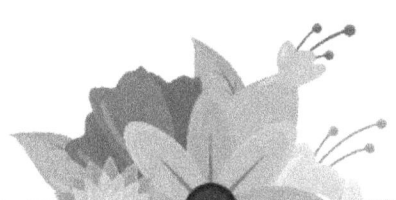

Enjoying this Notebook?

Please leave *Black Rose Press House* a review because we would love to know your thought, feedback, and opinions to create better products for you.
Please share how you creatively use your notebooks and journals.

THANKS
FOR YOUR SUPPORT

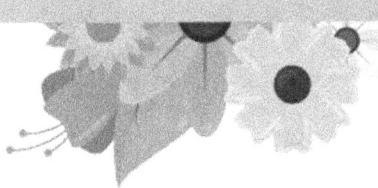

Scan This QR Code And Visit Our Author Page At-

amazon.com

www.ingramcontent.com/pod-product-compliance
Lightning Source LLC
Chambersburg PA
CBHW080530220526
45465CB00006B/2653